HIS KINGDOM YOUR PURPOSE

The Manual for Destiny and Transformation

by

DEREK SCHNEIDER

with

Joel Thornton

Kingdom®
publishing
Mansfield, Pennsylvania

© 2017 Derek Schneider

Published by:

Mansfield, Pennsylvania

P.O. Box 506
719 Lambs Creek Road
Mansfield, PA 16933

His Kingdom Your Purpose: The Manual for Destiny and
Transformation

ISBN-13: 978-1-883906-00-9
First Printing, January 2017

PRINTED IN THE UNITED STATES OF AMERICA

Table Of Contents

i

Dedication

I would like to dedicate this book and contents to Johnny and Juanita Berguson. Every so often God sends you lifelong friendships for the purpose of advancing the Kingdom and helping you grow as a person. Johnny and Juanita, you are a God-send and I am grateful for your faith, support, and dedication to the Kingdom in America and around the world.

Acknowledgements

I wish to acknowledge Dr. Sunday Adelaja for his unfailing mentoring that allows sons and daughters to grow and succeed.

Introduction

Understanding the Destiny and Transformation Mentorship Program "DTMP"

When you look at the mandate to disciple nations, you must see beyond just a revival or renewal and consider systemic societal change or societal transformation. Essentially for any people group or organization to rule a society, they must first establish systems within that society that help to accomplish a goal or establish a belief system within the minds of the people. Random evangelism is fine when it yields salvation, but when we talk about discipling a nation, we must embrace a systemic approach. Just as there can be systemic corruption within a country or region, the church can establish systemic righteousness. If the church wants to uproot systemic corruption, we must replace it with systemic righteousness, or as some would call it, organized righteousness.

Discipling nations is not the same as evangelism. Discipling a nation is different from person-to-person or even crusade evangelism. For example, crusade evangelism may save a lot of people in a particular country, but it does not necessarily transform the government, which is keeping that country in systemic corruption or systemic poverty. Truly discipling a nation requires a systemic approach or organized righteousness. This can look like various social initiatives that introduce Kingdom principles and Godly values being set up in a city or country. This can also look like a local church systematically placing Christian leaders into key places of influence in government. The systemic approach is not for the purpose of just witnessing, it is for the purpose of occupying.

A systemic approach dictated by the local church not only has the power to win people to Christ, but also has the power to transform the culture itself. When the culture begins to be transformed and begins to conform to the value system of Heaven, it is only a matter of time before more and more people want to meet the King whose values are so beneficial to the society. Therefore, we cannot think of discipling a nation unless we think in terms of the Church being an embassy of Heaven, promoting Kingdom values that transform culture in a systemic way.

It is very difficult, if not impossible, to disciple nations through Sunday morning church services alone. To fulfill the great commission that Jesus gave us, the church must utilize various intensive training and equipping models to produce real history makers. These key leaders, that are birthed within the local church, can strategically be placed in society to occupy crucial places of influence. In fact, as difficult as it may sound to some pastors, we must begin to explore the power of utilizing small groups of people for maximum societal influence. Typically, in the past we have thought that the bigger your church is, the more societal impact you will have. It is evident that this is just not so. Though a large church may be respected by the society around it, it is not merely the amount of people in a church that determines the direction of a society and the values it adheres to. This has been proven over and over again throughout history, when we see the mindsets and belief systems of whole cultures shifted by a small group of very dedicated individuals, rather than changed by the presence of a large church. As long as that small group of influencers remains dedicated and consistent, these cultural shifts generally happen over a period of time without the general population really recognizing it. In fact, in our own country (Canada) right now, various groups who work against the Kingdom of God are fighting systematically to change the laws of our country. After over a decade of pushing a very unholy agenda, they are achieving their goals. How is it possible that a small movement of people could actually influence a region or nation? In the New Testament, we saw how Jesus used a handful of men to transform the world, rather than establishing the Kingdom of God through a mega church in Jerusalem. Often we have thought that mobilizing 12 men to change the world became a reality because Jesus was the Son of God, but in actual fact, Jesus understood something very powerful about leveraging a few very dedicated individuals to impact culture.

On a small scale, I personally began to notice this principle at work a number of years ago in our own church. Over a period of ten years I witnessed how a group of radical young adults were able to bring great influence to the direction of the church vision and congregation at The Embassy. At that time, the Lord had spoken to me about not restricting the "new thing" that God was doing with a particular department or age group. By wisdom, humility, and the covering of our senior pastor, we watched a profound dynamic take place that made our church become very unique in the nation of Canada. Little did I realize that God was teaching me a very powerful principle about how any mass of people can be influenced by a small, dedicated, critical mass. In fact, I believe that for any local church to become apostolic or Kingdom-driven, it must begin to utilize small groups that initiate movements both within the church and beyond into society. A truly apostolic church or ministry center cannot expect to bring systemic change to a society or nation through Sunday morning services alone. We must give people various options and ministries to be a part of – as many options for ministry as there are societal problems or callings.

When we began holding History Makers Trainings on a more frequent basis, this powerful concept began to emerge in an even more effective and clear way. We kept the crowds of each training to a maximum of 30 people to avoid the "conference style." This allowed us to apply maximum focus and attention on the total transformation of these 30 people. What we saw was extraordinary. In a small group environment, where the attendees were completely submitted to the choreography and goal of the program, the power of genuine intensive training could be seen. In a short period of time, not only did we see these individuals radically transformed, but for most of them the fruitfulness and influence that exploded from their lives after the training remained. They saw amazing doors suddenly begin to open for Kingdom influence in society. Now, after more than two years of holding History Makers Trainings, the power of applied pressure and intensive trainings to produce results beyond the four walls of the church has become undoubtedly evident. The majority of those who have taken the training have gone on to become very effective and influential leaders in their fields. Despite years of faithful church attendance and a heart to be effective for Jesus, they are seeing results they never saw before the training.

The idea of leveraging a small group of highly trained leaders is what also gave birth to what we call the "Transformation Council" concept.

Once we began to see the results coming from the History Makers Training and the small group dynamic, I took up the challenge of starting a series of small groups called "Transformation Councils." Not only has this model worked powerfully for us in Canada, but through it, we were able to reach close to 250,000 people globally in under two years time. I believe it is based on Biblical principles and is a strategy that can be reproduced in any local church, organization, city, or nation.

On Sunday mornings, for three months, I began to advertise a Destiny and Transformation Mentorship Program (DTMP) inviting the congregation to a preliminary meeting. We promoted this group as a movement for people who want to effect change in society and felt called to ministry outside of the church. We had approximately 120 in attendance for the first meeting - most of these were graduates of our three-day History Makers Training.

For the next eight months, we met weekly and I taught on the Kingdom of God, societal transformation principles, church reformation principles, and much more. The teachings given at those weekly meetings were not your typical Sunday morning messages, and the meetings often were quite lengthy. We also brought in guest speakers who specialized on such topics as destiny, identity, and calling.

On a typical Mentorship night, we began with prayer for the region, then teaching and training, then open discussion, and sometimes more prayer on into the night. These weekly meetings were intensive and intentionally so. On top of all of that, at the end of each meeting, homework (we called them "activation points") was distributed and due to be handed in sometime the following week. The homework was based on the message and concepts being taught. Assignments were graded and marks were given. Over the eight-month period of training, myself and the DTMP administration kept a very detailed record of attendance, grading, and understanding of calling and "heart" of each individual. The attendees were aware of this and welcomed the challenge of growing. After all, they were the ones who showed up in the first place and this was a "training and equipping" concept within our church where it was okay to have weighty expectations. This was not a Sunday morning service, and these were not new believers. They were those who had signed up to bring the Kingdom of God to a very secular society. These were soldiers in training!

Once we all understood this fact, there was a lot of freedom to challenge, develop, and train these leaders in an environment designed not to just "inspire" them, but also to transform them.

Keeping record of attendance, and tracking individual performance and dedication was to apply pressure towards their growth. It was also because by the end of this 18-week intensive training, those who remained faithful and committed were put into a group (or groups if there are more than 12). These groups of no more than 12 to 15 people were called Transformation Councils.

These were chosen based on the results of consistent attendance, homework assignments, and understanding of calling and real heart. Not only would they go on to further training and community, but they would also immediately be able to establish social programs and ministries in the community, pursue government grants, and work towards becoming major influencers in their sphere of calling.

These Transformation Council meetings were a milestone for me in ministry and were very special. Within the first few weeks of holding them, the meetings became hugely dynamic to the point that many outsiders would come wanting to take part. With all the immediate excitement over the new movement, we were careful not to turn it into another church service. We wanted to focus on a small group "intensive" dynamic.

Each week as we met together, the atmosphere was incredible. At times there were tears. Sometimes, prayer was electric with the Presence of God. Other times there was strategizing as to the next steps towards community and national influence. The Transformation Council Movement was a critical mass that stepped into the fires of an eight-month transformation tank and came out equipped to "Go." The testimonies of many of those who went through the eight-month training are amazing. Some of them had attended church their whole lives yet never knew their purpose, wondering when God would begin to use them. Often there were tears of joy as they would stand in the meetings and share about how this new model had given them courage to believe that God can use them. From their lips, the transformation in their lives was evident, but even more amazing was how evident it was in their faces and personalities. These people had been re-wired for high performance ministry and became different people! As a pastor, this brought me joy beyond measure.

These kinds of meetings never created a negative stir within the church or became a hindrance to the Sunday morning service. They complimented and enhanced the vision of our church. After all, it is very powerful on a Sunday morning during your sermon about making disciples to bring a group like that on to the stage to present their ministries. It is even more powerful to hand them a microphone and let them share what their ministry is, the solutions they are bringing to society, and how many people they plan to reach in the next year. This kind of preaching makes theory a reality and is one of the best ways to shift the mindset of your local church. Amazingly, some of these key leaders are now developing curricula and being invited to speak about their ministry in other places.

When we first began, some questioned whether it was a problem that many had transitioned out or stepped away, but I always reminded them that we were not trying to build a church or hold more services. Rather, we were trying to narrow down who the core dedicated ones were and then train them for maximum societal impact.

Essentially, through this systematic approach, we were able to call together some of the highest potential leaders from our church, those who were sitting there the whole time never realizing the potential they had. Those who, even I, had not realized their potential. Through this model, we would train them, equip them, and send them out to occupy territory and bring change to a community. Not only has this deepened the understanding of our own church body on societal transformation, but it is beginning to impact the mindset of various community leaders. Those in secular society trying to do community work desire real networking and partnership, and the Transformation Council concept gave our church a profound presence and influence in the community.

If there is a problem in society that needs solving, we do not just preach about it from the pulpit, we form a small group, apply pressure to them through training and equipping, and release them to solve that particular problem in society. We form councils to strategize how to occupy key positions in society and bring Kingdom values and influence to it. We apply pressure to small groups much like seeds. As we become fruitful and multiply by God's grace, we begin to fill society with both the life and the lifestyle of the Kingdom of God, subduing it for His glory.

-    Derek Schneider

All Scripture references in this book are from the New American Standard Bible (1995 Updated Version), unless otherwise noted differently. The New American Standard Bible is commonly abbreviated as NASB and published by The Lockman Foundation, LaHabra, CA.

SECTION ONE:

UNDERSTANDING YOUR CALLING AND PURPOSE

CHAPTER ONE:

HELL WAS NOT MADE FOR YOU

Genesis 1:26-27 is the beginning of mankind, how it all started, the original intention, the original purpose.

Genesis 1:26-27

Then God said, "Let Us make man in Our image, according to Our likeness; and let them rule over the fish of the sea and over the birds of the sky and over the cattle and over all the earth, and over every creeping thing that creeps on the earth." God created man in His own image, in the image of God He created him; male and female He created them.

God made you in *His* image and likeness. **IMAGE** is actually speaking about nature, attributes, and characteristics. He made us in His image. When the Bible says, *'Let us make man in our image and likeness,'* **LIKENESS** is referring to function or action. We are not only to look like God; we are to *act* like God. That is powerful! God, who exists as King in the Heavenly realm, and made a prototype of Heaven in the form of the earth. He made a little Heaven, the Garden of Eden, a place where God's glory was concentrated, and then essentially He said, *"As I rule in Heaven, I'm going to put a prototype of Me, My image and likeness, to rule in that garden."* That is who you are. God actually made man in His image and likeness.

God created man in His image. Wow! In the image of God, He created him, male and female, He created them. God made you to look like Him! God made you to talk like Him. God made you to act like Him. God delighted in making you, His image, His representative and He made you perfect. He knitted you together in your mother's womb. He created you in His image. When you see a lame person, a diseased person, a person depressed and bound up by the enemy, you are looking at someone who was made in the image of God, but this fallen world has crippled that person. They are, however, still made in the image and likeness of God.

What could we do if we really lived like we were created in the image and likeness of God?

A wise man once said, "If you want to change a nation, take about twelve people that nobody thinks could ever amount to anything, let the Gospel of the Kingdom work through them, and that *entire* nation will hear about it." And that is what he did. Pastor Sunday Adelaja took seven alcoholics and drug addicts, and taught them the Gospel of the Kingdom and watched their lives transform. One person was an alcoholic named Natasha; she called herself "Natasha Alcoholic" because that is all she knew herself to be and felt that was all she was good for – drinking. She came to the Church (which started as a Bible study with seven people) and did not understand a thing, but felt some sense of joy. Here, she gave her life to the Lord. The Church grew to 30,000 people, and she wrote the book, **When You Can't Live and Can't Die**, and started hundreds of rehab centers throughout Ukraine and the world – what God can do with somebody! We have to see people this way!

Genesis 2:15

Then the Lord God took the man and put him into the Garden of Eden to cultivate it and keep it. MANAge / ministry.

Whenever you do not know the purpose of something, abuse is inevitable. Whenever you do not know why something exists, you will abuse it. We have to understand the purpose of

4

mankind. We are not here to wait and get by until we get to Heaven. We are here to have a relationship with God on Earth and to excel in some sphere of influence. Whether or not it is family or business, we are to rule and excel and to bring glory to God.

This relationship that Adam and Eve, the very first man and the first woman, had with God was so very deep. It was a communion with God that was awesome. They loved to be in His presence. They walked together in the cool of the day, they knew God closely. God put them in the Garden to cultivate it and work it. It is critical that you understand that mankind was made for two things.   *Purpose*

① Number one: you were designed to have fellowship with God. You were not born just to fulfill some kind of religious duties. You were not designed to beg a God that is so far away that you cannot reach Him. No! Man was designed to walk with God in intimacy, and closeness. That is what we were made to do. To know Him intimately.

② Man was also made with a second purpose. That purpose is to "work (or manage) the garden." What is your garden? Where is your garden? That is the question every person must answer for themselves if they are going to live a fulfilled life. What is my purpose? To what sphere of society or realm of influence have I been called?

What is my garden? Once you find your garden you have to effectively manage your garden. To take care of it, to rule it. To bring The Kingdom of God to that garden. Every person was made to walk with God, to fellowship with Him and to manage their garden.

Where is your sphere of influence or what is your garden? Where is the sphere that God has placed you in, to bring Him into? Satan came and deceived Adam and Eve in the Garden.

Genesis 3:4-6 says, "But the serpent said to the woman, 'You will not surely die. For God knows that when you eat of it your eyes will be opened, and you will be like God, knowing good and evil.'" The great deception and trickery of Satan was the fact that Adam and Eve were already like God. Satan essentially tempted Eve with the opportunity to become like God through sin. It seems he still uses this tactic today. Somehow Satan has been able to convince the world that sin will make them great.

Adam and Eve had an intimacy with God that was unfathomable. Adam and Eve were close with God and when they sinned, they exchanged their relationship and closeness with God for a lie. They became wanderers, lost, and separated from God.

Now, Adam and Eve had incredible fellowship with the Lord, intimacy that is just unfathomable in our current state. Imagine the height of a worship experience that you have had, where you felt the presence of God so deeply, so wonderfully, around you. They had that ecstasy on a daily basis. Once sin entered into the picture, however, the glory of that garden and the glory that Adam and Eve experienced, was lost. At that point mankind was doomed to one thing – a place called hell.

We have probably all heard many awful descriptions of hell, and Biblically we know that this place of fire is real. The real tragedy of hell, however, is not necessarily fire, or the burning. It is eternal separation from fellowship with God.

We do not have the ability to truly understand the reality of the absence of God. You see, even as horrible as life can be on earth, the earth still experiences the presence of God. While it may appear that God is absent, and He often appears to be absent from the horrors of this world, God is still present in this earth. So, we must understand the absolute decay and depravity that will occur in a place that cannot – ever – have the presence of God, a place called hell, where God will never visit. He will never intervene in life in hell. This is the one place in the entire universe where God's presence is never experienced.

This means that sin will abound. With sin will come the depravity of the soul that is darkened and has no light from Heaven in it. With sin will come the torment of knowing that there is no hope of redemption. There is no hope that tomorrow will be a better day.

The trouble is the concept is hard to understand. It is hard to understand because, even for the atheist God is still present. Wanting God to not exist does make Him not exist. Declaring that God is dead, has never existed, does not make it true. So, in the world envisioned by the atheist God still exists. He still works to improve the plight of mankind. That cannot and does not happen in hell.

Hell is eternal separation from God. All while we exist in the understanding that God is alive, God is good, and God is removed from our reality. The Bible says that every knee shall bow to the name of Jesus. Before a person is cast into hell they will know that Jesus is the Son of God, God is real, and they are not in His presence – ever again.

So, for one brief, shining moment every human who has ever lived will be in the glorious presence of God. Some will be ushered into His kingdom to experience His presence forever. Others will be forced from His presence to spend eternity separated from the God of the Universe, who they know exists and reached out to them throughout their time on earth.

Now, that is true horror that is unimaginable in its reality!

Understanding the horror of hell is critical to properly serving your community. Only then can we see the value God places on mankind and truly see every person's potential. When we interact with people, no matter who they are, no matter how

See people to their potential not their present state.
Always come from a place of love.

much they may have done to us, no matter how much they may irritate us, we have to see these people according to their potential and not their present state. You may want to call people *bad*, and may want nothing to do with them. The nature of God is to focus on what they will become, not who they are. God is loving enough to walk *you* through that process. We all have a story. Likewise, God is loving enough to walk them through that same process!

We cannot even begin to talk about reaching people if we do not have a revelation of what God thinks of them. Otherwise we will build a ministry in our image to make us look good and it will not be about people. It will use people, but it will not be about them.

You cannot do anything beyond the four walls of the Church that will really be effective, unless it flows from a place of genuine and sacrificial love.

While on earth, God is working on us and trying to get our attention and we can feel His presence at times. When you are in hell, however, you are separated from God forever. That was never His intention for you. You were made in His image. And so, mankind was lost and needed a Savior and we know that the Bible says, God sent His son, Jesus – God's express image and likeness. When Jesus came, He walked the earth and He died on a cross and He paid the price for your sins. Why?

So that you could have fellowship with God, again. Intimacy. You see, the veil in the Temple of Solomon kept the sinner back and separated from God. It was a big veil that separated people from God. When Jesus died on the cross, the veil was torn in two (Matthew 27:51). This is a reality that symbolizes the fact that we now have entrance into the Garden of Eden lifestyle with Jesus again.

hell was originally made for the devil & angels.

Anyone can have it. Not only can you have fellowship with God, you can now bring God's power to earth. You can now work your garden, cultivate your sphere of influence, and cause Jesus to reign. Jesus does not have to come back and rule the earth, He rules the earth through you.

Now, think about John 3:16.

John 3:16

For God so loved the world, that He gave His only begotten Son, that whoever believes in Him shall not perish, but have eternal life.

What is the urgency to keep people from perishing that we are talking about? To perish is to be lost and separated from God in a place called hell.

Look in the book of Matthew 25:41. What does the Bible have to say about hell?

Matthew 25:41

Then He will also say to those on His left, "Depart from Me, accursed ones, into the eternal fire which has been prepared for the devil and his angels;"

In verse 41, Jesus is speaking about the judgment that the lost will receive. He's talking about when He returns what will happen to people who have rejected Him.

hell

Hell was not made for you! According to Jesus, hell was made for the devil and his angels. The eternal fire, the place of burning, the place of being lost, was not made for you. Now, let's see what the book of Jude has to say about hell.

Jude 1:7 *Sodom & Gomorrah — Hell*
— city destroyed by fire

...Just as Sodom and Gomorrah and the cities around them, since they in the same way as these indulged in gross immorality and went after strange flesh, are exhibited as an example in undergoing the punishment of eternal fire.

What does that mean, as an example? What happened to Sodom and Gomorrah? They were destroyed by fire. The Bible is saying that they are an example to us of something. God is trying to hint something to us. It says, "Just as an example, in undergoing the punishment of eternal fire." There really is an eternal fire that burns. That was not designed for you and me to go to but was designed for Satan and his angels.

Luke 13:28-29

In that place there will be weeping and gnashing of teeth when you see Abraham and Isaac and Jacob and all the prophets in the kingdom of God, but yourselves being thrown out. And they will come from east and west and from north and south, and will recline at the table in the kingdom of God.

I can think of some people I know, who died, but they did not know Jesus and have been burning for years in hell, right now as we speak. They have only been burning for a few years and we have not even hit eternity yet! Oh, the horrible awesomeness of this place. But it was not made for you.

There are a lot of people who claim to have had experiences where they have died and gone to hell and have come back and given their lives over to God. One particular gentleman has an incredible story of how he died, went to hell or had a vision, where God took him there, and he now speaks globally. He is an amazing person. He has churches around the world asking him to come and speak to them. He has a good marriage, is well respected, and every phrase he says, he has Scripture to back it up. He describes his experience in a way that is fascinating. His wife found him in the middle of the night curled up on the floor weeping in terror. He described hell as being a place where there is no air; the stench is so bad that when you are trying to breathe, all you can do is choke while trying to draw breath. He described the thirst that you feel and tells of the Scripture where the rich man begs Lazarus to get a drop of water for his tongue because he was so thirsty from the heat, from the flames (Luke 16:19-31).

This man said that you are literally so desperate for water to drink, and you do not ever get it. He also spoke about the fact that you suffer from so much agony and that there is cannibalism, because you are trying to eat your own flesh so that you can actually die, because you find no rest. He also discussed the torment that the demons are inflicting on you there, because of their love of defacing the image and likeness of God. The demons love to bring destruction to you because they believe they are doing it to God.

Luke 16:24

And he cried out and said, "Father Abraham, have mercy on me, and send Lazarus so that he may dip the tip of his finger in water and cool off my tongue, for I am in agony in this flame."

Thank God this place was not prepared for you. This place of weeping and gnashing of teeth.

There is one aspect of hell that is very, very crucial to know – hell is not bad because of all it contains. What actually makes hell so gruelling for the people who go there is that they know that they are **eternally** separated from God. **_The worst thing about hell is the eternal separation from fellowship with God_**. What we want to do with society is cause them to return to their Father; to return to their original image and to be restored before it is too late.

11

When we go back to the beginning, to the fall of man and the original sin, we can see how much God loves us. Once mankind sinned, God began a process for saving us. Aren't we glad Jesus came to solve the problem of separation from God? When Jesus died on the cross, the veil was torn in two. This is symbolic of the fact that now we have entrance to Heaven and can have a relationship with God. If you have come through Jesus Christ, you are with the Father. No man can come to the Father, but through the Son. If you have come through the Son, you are with the Father. If you need some presence of God, just open your hands and get to know Papa God. You have been brought into relationship; you have been brought to that type of Eden where you can walk in closeness with Him. Not everybody has that, but we have that!

Mark 9:43-48

If your hand causes you to stumble, cut it off; it is better for you to enter life crippled, than, having your two hands, to go into hell, into the unquenchable fire, [where THEIR WORM DOES NOT DIE, AND THE FIRE IS NOT QUENCHED.] If your foot causes you to stumble, cut it off; it is better for you to enter life lame than to have your two feet and be cast into hell; [where THEIR WORM DOES NOT DIE AND THE FIRE IS NOT QUENCHED.] If your eye causes you to stumble, throw it out, for it is better for you to enter the kingdom of God with one eye, than, having two eyes, to be cast into hell, where THEIR WORM DOES NOT DIE, AND THE FIRE IS NOT QUENCHED.

What an alarming and peculiar passage! Now, is Jesus saying that if you sin with your right hand that you should cut your right hand off? NO! Because a lot of us would come back next week without hands, feet, eyes, ears. Jesus is giving us a picture or an analogy. Jesus is using extreme illustrations to get our attention on the magnitude of how serious and awful sin is! He is trying to get our attention that hell is real and you do not want to go there! Jesus is trying to say that hell is so bad that a person should be willing to take any measure to avoid going there, and this means avoiding sin completely!

He also says, *"...where the worm does not die..."* The actual term there is **maggot**. Maggots are fascinating. The more they eat, the sooner they die. Consumption is what actually kills them, so when Jesus talks about hell being a place where the maggots do not die, it means they continually feast on your flesh. This is reality.

We were not made for hell. Human beings were not made to go there. We are the ones who have the gift of salvation, but the world does not know this or they have heard it, but have become numb to it. Whether they know it or not, hell is not a place they want to go, and we can rescue them from that consequence of sin!

While we are on earth, we have the opportunity to call on God and be saved. You have years of your life to call on His Name and He will respond to you. But there comes a time when even God Himself will not respond to you – and that place is hell. You were not made for that place. You were made in the image and likeness of God Almighty! You were made to excel in society and establish the Kingdom of God.

We, as believers, must understand our purpose in this life. We are to rescue people from an eternity separated from God! You have been rescued, but they have not.

Have you ever been driving down the street and you say, I wonder if that person knows Jesus? This is where every soul counts.

I grew up a pastor's kid. I felt I really knew the Lord. But I discovered that I really did not know Him PERSONALLY – I just knew "about" Him.

As a young teenager and drummer, I had the opportunity to tour with my Jazz band for a short season. One morning when preparing to leave for a particular show I found myself praying, "Lord protect me today." I did not know why I had prayed that prayer and it is true, you never know when your time to die will come. Foolishly, I never wore my seatbelt the whole morning going from place to place. It was almost mid-afternoon when a few of the band members and I came out of a restaurant and got into the car. Coincidentally, I put my seat belt on for the first time the whole morning. As we were pulling out onto the road there was a car that was turning in so that the driver could not see that in the other lane a van was racing towards us, obviously speeding. The police who arrived on the scene later affirmed this. From where I was sitting I was actually the only person who could see and anticipate the collision that was about to occur. But I became so gripped with fear that I could not say stop to the driver. The driver pulled out. This speeding vehicle drove right into my side of the car – right into me! I do not remember a lot about what took place as my head went right through the side window! I just remember being frightened and being shocked. Then, everything was dark. Amidst the blackness I could just faintly see a very tall figure standing in the right side of my vision, with huge shoulders almost like a football player. This being must have been close to nine or ten feet tall. I could not see his face; I just saw an outline. I knew he was standing there looking at me. I believe to this day that it was an angel. It is difficult to try and describe this in human terms but I knew I was somewhere not of this world. And there was Heaven and there was hell before me.

Immediately I had an overwhelming sense of horror about where I might end up and how I might spend eternity. As this experience dragged on (for how long I do not know) I knew that I would be lost if I were to die that day. The next part is a blur, but my friend who was in the car behind, said I got out and wandered around the road, dripping in blood! It reminded me of a scene from a horror movie. I could not remember a thing. All I knew was that I felt the presence of God strong around me. The strongest I had ever felt it in my life. The ambulance attendant came and he asked if I remembered where I was sitting. I tried so hard to remember, but I could not remember. I had amnesia. He put me in the ambulance and as I laid there I remembered my name, that was it. I said, "My name is Derek Schneider and I spoke with God!" This of course did not impress the ambulance attendants.

Once we arrived at the hospital I was there alone in the room, and began to weep in the Presence of God. Not because I was scared, but because I began to feel the Presence of God lifting again and things were returning to normal. I did not want that wonderful very real presence to go.

I realized that the devil, if he could take your life, he would. He hates you! He hates your image! Because you look like the Son of God who kicked him out of Heaven! You look like the ruler! He does not want rulers on the earth. He does not see your little sins and shortcomings. He sees your potential. He knows what you will do. So he has got to take you out now. It hit me that the devil hates me and he hates you.

The devil makes **no** distinction. Satan is out to steal and kill, and wants to destroy anyone and everyone. Satan seeks to destroy God's image. He does not care how effective or ineffective you are. He wants to have a literal holocaust of human beings. The devil is everything disgusting. He is poverty. He is disease. He is depravity. He is tears and sorrow. He is drug addiction. He is destruction incarnate, and he wants to destroy mankind. But God came in the flesh to bring judgment to that serpent – that old snake – and Satan thought he had Jesus defeated, but Jesus was just reproducing Himself in all of us. We carry something incredible!

Why? Because of your purpose! Because of your destiny!

He does not want you to achieve it. If he can take you out, he will.

There is a hell and you are not meant to go there. I want you to think about the people in your sphere of influence who do not know the Lord. The reality of eternity is what you need to catch. *The only way you will work hard enough and make the sacrifices necessary to reach a community is when you have eternity in mind.* You must have the genuine compassion of Jesus and a genuine love for people. You need to have the reality of souls. For the joy set before Him, Jesus endured the cross to set many captives free and to lead many sons to glory.

Activation Points:

1. Give a definition of what it means to be "made according to His image and likeness."

2. Describe how God has created us to function on the earth. Based on this chapter what was God's original intent?

3. Give a thorough description of what hell is actually like. What makes it such a horrible place?

4. Give a thorough explanation of Mark 9:43-48. What does this passage mean?

5. How did reading this chapter make you feel? Are the any practical changes you want to make in your life? What are they?

CHAPTER TWO:

GOD'S DREAM: YOUR MISSION

SoN: Study the Word + WAlK out it out
PRAYER LIFE - Respect the growth process

Many people do not know that God has a dream, that He has a passion, and that He actually has desires. Did you know that God actually is not satisfied? God is not satisfied and that is our problem! That is a problem for us because He has a way of seeking out to save that which was lost.

We know that Galatians 4 deals with sonship, understanding what it means to be a son in the Kingdom. What is needed to be a son? You need to study the Word and not just listen to it, or hear it, but walk out the Word in your everyday life. You need to have a prayer life and do what you see God doing and bear God's image on the earth. Sons and daughters know how to make sure that they receive an inheritance from the Father. We have to respect the growth process to really become a son or a daughter.

What are children like in the Kingdom as compared to mature sons and daughters? Children are selfish and selfishness is a great problem in our society, especially in the church. Children are born and sons are given or sown into the harvest. **A son or daughter is entrusted with responsibility, they have a job to do, and they are expected to reap the harvest and bring back a reward for the Father.** Sons and daughters are entrusted with the harvest and are expected to bring the harvest in. They present the harvest before God; a harvest of souls.

Children are born; sons are given

Galatians 4:1-7

Now I say, as long as the heir is a child, he does not differ at all from a slave although he is owner of everything, but he is under guardians and managers until the date set by the father. So also we, while we were children, were held in bondage under the elemental things of the world. But when the fullness of the time came, God sent forth His Son, born of a woman, born under the Law, so that He might redeem those who were under the Law, that we might receive the adoption as sons. Because you are sons, God has sent forth the Spirit of His Son into our hearts, crying, 'Abba! Father!' Therefore you are no longer a slave, but a son; and if a son, then an heir through God.

So in Galatians 4 we understand that sons and daughters are entrusted with an inheritance, this is an important concept to understand. **The inheritance of sons and daughters is actually their purpose, calling, and destiny.** The inheritance of a son or daughter is their destiny.

You have been put on this planet for a reason. You are not here by accident; do not let your being here be in vain. No matter who you are, no matter what your past is, you are here at this time, this year, this age, for a reason, not just to pass the time. In fact, no matter how old you are, if there is breath in your body, if you are alive, you are responsible to give life. **If you are alive, you are responsible to give life,** whether you are in a wheelchair, whether in your hospital bed dying, as long as you are breathing in that bed, that nurse should run into God when she or he comes in to take care of you. As long as you have life, you are responsible to give life.

You are a conduit of Heaven while you are on earth. We are life-giving spirits. God created you and when it says He made man, He made him to have a life-speaking spirit and a life-giving spirit. You are here because you are to give life. Once you

As long as you have life you are to give life the spirit of God

received salvation, you were expected to give life as *He* gave life. You are expected to be a conduit of that life.

Saving souls bringing life.

Because I have life, I *give life*. You may not be able to define your calling or purpose. You may not be able to define what your destiny is. Yet, because of the very fact that you are alive and breathing, it means you have a destiny and you have a mission to give life. Even if you do not know what the details are, write it down, I must give life, no matter what the details are. Sons and daughters know their inheritance is their destiny. Your destiny and purpose is always connected to others. It is always connected to souls and soul winning. Your destiny is always connected to people and giving life to people. If you feel your purpose is to be a consumer of money, fame, and power and your purpose is not an outflow of God's life, you have not stepped into your inheritance. That is why you can be a world famous artist, make a lot of money, have great fame, and even influence people, and then you die and end up not getting into Heaven because you did not receive Christ and make Jesus your Lord. Therefore, you do not have an inheritance.

We *all* have a purpose and calling. And so we have to be careful how we look at *others* and *ourselves*. It is imperative that we do not judge people, but that we actually see them the way God sees them.

We must become life-giving spirits. ***In order to give life, we have a responsibility to have life***. That is why you are laboring in the Word and in prayer and keeping a heart postured toward people. It is not just laboring in prayer, but it is about posturing your heart everyday towards people.

As a son or daughter of God, you are a prince or a princess by bloodline. You may not always feel like it, but because you are a son of God you are a prince, which means you were born to excel in some aspect of life. The very fact that there is breath in your body and you are still alive means you are responsible to

Lead → bring justice to earth.

give life. ***But more than that, a prince or a princess gives rulership***. Now when we say rule, we are not talking about lording our will over another person's. We are talking about excelling, leadership, and bringing justice. We are talking about establishing the kingdom and its influence. We are talking about ruling in the areas where God has given you influence and abilities. People see God in your excellence. Mercy must also be a part of your leadership.

You do these things because *God* does those things. God is excellent at everything He does. God brings justice everywhere He goes. God is merciful. God is the ultimate Leader. His Kingdom is the one true Kingdom. Therefore, His sons and daughters, as kings and judges of this earth and as He rules in Heaven, we are to rule on this earth. You were born to rule and excel in something as a son or daughter.

Pre Cross

Because we are sons and daughters, we are responsible to fulfill God's dream. So what is God's dream? Prior to Jesus going to the cross, what was God's dream? Amazingly according to Matthew 5:6 you could say that God's dream was restricted to the house of Israel alone. So what was this "pre-cross commission?"

Matthew 10:5-8

These twelve Jesus sent out after instructing them: "Do not go in the way of the Gentiles, and do not enter any city of the Samaritans; but rather go to the lost sheep of the house of Israel. And as you go, preach, saying, 'The kingdom of Heaven is at hand.' Heal the sick, raise the dead, cleanse the lepers, cast out demons. Freely you received, freely give.

Notice that prior to the cross the emphasis was on the house of Israel, miracles, and the casting out of demons only. Once Jesus was raised from the dead, however, He gave us a wonderful new commission called the Great Commission. And it is called that for a reason!

Matthew 28:18-20 *Great Commission Post Cross.*

And Jesus came up and spoke to them, saying, "All authority has been given to Me in Heaven and on earth. Go therefore and make disciples of all the nations, baptizing them in the name of the Father and the Son and the Holy Spirit, teaching them to observe all that I commanded you; and lo, I am with you always, even to the end of the age."

Prior

God purchased the earth with His own blood. Prior to the cross, the pre-cross Commission we call it, He sent out the disciples to put a dent in the devil's camp through the Gospel of the Kingdom, and through miracles, healings, signs, and wonders. After the cross, the post-cross Commission, Jesus said now that I have died, *all* authority in Heaven and on earth is mine. *Post* Therefore, now *you* go fulfill My dream. That is what He essentially said. God purchased the earth with His own blood and now God has total jurisdiction over the earth, the only problem is He is not here, so He gave us the keys and the title deed, He has something for us to do. **God has a dream; therefore, we have a mission.**

Exousia-

When Jesus said all authority has been given unto Me, the Greek word there is *exousia. Exousia* means, "power to act, to control, or to have dominion, jurisdiction, liberty, or the right to act." Jesus is saying all the earth has been paid for by His blood and He has dominion there. So *exousia* means God has delegated all authority to His Son, Jesus.

Essentially *authority means the right to rule.* What Jesus said was, now that I have gone to the cross, and have been raised from the dead, authority in Heaven and on earth is Mine! On the basis of this authority GO! And establish the Kingdom of God wherever I send you – and teach them to observe! Jesus bought the earth and the currency He used was His blood. Jesus bought back the earth. God bought back the earth through the death of His Son. God said, I gave up My Son for the exchange of the earth. He is above *all* authority. Jesus Christ, now has the right to rule over all the earth; not the desire, the right.

So look what happens in Luke 10:17, it's very simple, yet profound.

Luke 10:17-20

The seventy returned with joy, saying, "Lord, even the demons are subject to us in Your name." And He said to them, "I was watching Satan fall from Heaven like lightning. Behold, I have given you authority [exousia] to tread on serpents and scorpions, and over all the power of the enemy, and nothing will injure you. Nevertheless, do not rejoice in this, that the spirits are subject to you, but rejoice that your names are recorded in Heaven." in the lambs book.

So Jesus sent out His disciples, He wanted them to establish the Kingdom of God on the earth because He paid for it. The 70 returned to Him saying, "Even the demons are subject to us because of Your name." So the God-given authority that they were given, or the right to rule, which was given to Jesus from the Father, because it was the Father who made the transaction and purchase, that delegated authority has now been delegated to *you.*

It says, *"Behold, I have given you authority [exousia] to tread on serpents and scorpions, and over all the power of the enemy, and nothing will injure you. Nevertheless, do not rejoice in this, that the spirits are subject to you, but rejoice that your names are recorded in Heaven."*

God rules the earth through delegated authority. He delegated it to Jesus, and Jesus delegated it to you. ***You have the right to***

rule on earth. You have the right to bring justice to society. You have the right to bring mercy to society. *"As Jesus was"* when He on the earth, you now have a right to be.

It is not too strong to say that you are expected to bring justice. You are expected to bring mercy. You are expected to rule on the earth. It is not enough to merely have a right, we must exercise the rights we have. If we do not exercise these rights, we are in danger of being a clanging cymbal. 1 Cor. 1-13.

Now I want to explain that concept to you because we think it is just summed up with the name of Jesus. We say, "In the name of Jesus let Toronto [or your city] be saved." We think it is just using the name Jesus and demons will be cast out. Well, I have gone to Mexico and I have met a lot of men named Jesus there! Just by mentioning their names of course demons are not leaving someone's body. It is not just the pronunciation of the name of Jesus, it is a type of faith *in* the name of Jesus. It is an understanding. It is a knowing – an assurance.

Let me explain to you what it means to function in the name of Jesus. This is essential if you are going to go into society, if you are going to bring Kingdom influence. What is God's dream? ***God's dream is that we would go and disciple nations, so that we would lay claim to what He has already paid for.***

Demonstration:

Pretend I bought you a car. I cannot go to the dealership, you have to go down to the dealership and get it yourself. When you go down to the dealership you walk in and they say to you, what are you doing here? And you answer, "Actually I own that car" (and point to a car). So the dealer checks the paperwork and they confirm that the car was purchased for you. So, you have the right to drive that car off the lot because somebody purchased it. You fulfilled my dream. You went and got the car.

Power of Attorney   POA
Put a demand on myself to get Jesus' results.

That is what God wants us to do. He already bought it, now He wants us to go and lay claim to it. He already bought that region. He already bought those drug addicts. He already bought those business people. He already bought those CEOs. He already bought those students. He already bought those seniors. He bought that education system. He bought that government agency. He bought that media outlet. What is stopping us from going and getting them? You thought you did not have the right. You thought Jesus still needed to do something, but He already bought them. Get your life right and go get them and bring them to the feet of Jesus. Bring them as your inheritance.

P. O A

So here is what it means to come in the name of Jesus. It is called the power of attorney. ***The power of attorney is the legal right to act in proxy on behalf of another; legal authority.***

Essentially, when you come in the name of somebody, you have the right to do in that situation, what he or she would do if they were present. That is why the demons were driven out. "All authority in Heaven and on earth has been given to Me, therefore *you go* in *My* name." Meaning, you have the right to do, you have the right to go to nations in Jesus' name, and do what He would do if He were there. That is what it means to go in His name. So whether I say the name of Jesus or not, I am telling that demon to get out, and when he sees me, he sees the Father. Even before I say something he is squirming because I have come in the Name. Because I put a demand on myself to get the results Jesus would, if He were in my shoes. I take responsibility for my sphere and I rule as Jesus would if He were there. We do not sign up to be in the ministry, we sign up to be Jesus.

Therefore, I try to treat people the way *Jesus* would. I am bearing His image as a Son. We must want to be like Jesus and get His results. He wants to gather up every sphere of society and every realm of life, but He needs *you* to go do it. And He says here is My name. You go in My name. It is about ownership and it's about His Kingdom coming through you and me.

*Disciples rejoiced because the demons were subject to them * your name is written in heaven*

Now look at what happened with the disciples. Luke says that they came back rejoicing. Why did they come back rejoicing? They came back rejoicing because the demons were subject to them. Jesus' reply to them, however, had nothing to do with the defeat of Satan, but it had everything to do with rejoicing because their names were written in Heaven. That is to say, it is always about Heavenly registration. It is always about souls. He is saying, yes you are fulfilling your destiny but *always* remember that it is about your name being written in Heaven. At the end of the day that is what it is about.

Luke 10:19

Behold, I have given you authority to tread on serpents and scorpions, and over all the power of the enemy, and nothing will injure you.

What does this look like in settings outside of the local church? What does it look like in your educational system? What does it look like at a trustee meeting? Can you stand up and say, "I have all authority over every unclean spirit in the school and I am trampling on scorpions?" You would be thrown out of the door! How do you bring that kind of authority and give it over to God?

When Jesus brought Kingdom principles into what He was doing, like showing love and mercy, He was actually judging. This is how you bring God 's judgment. Judgment is not necessarily calling down fire on someone or something. When we talk about having authority over all of these things, we are talking about bringing God's justice; bringing God's judgment. *Judgment is this, "bringing to order, that which was in chaos."* In other words, every time I function in the opposite spirit, I am actually *judging* the opposing spirit. I am doing what Jesus would do, if He were in my shoes.

Examples:

- You are downtown, go to a homeless shelter, and give someone a meal. You judged the spirit of poverty. And you are establishing the rule and righteousness of God.
- You take in a single mom who is unable to pay her rent. You judged *that* spirit of poverty.
- You, as a business person, choose to do business honestly while others are cutting corners and committing fraud. You have judged the spirit of greed and dishonesty.
- You take a group of young people to bless and honor national leaders. How do you do this if what some of them represent is terrible? The church in the past has cursed them. We have retreated from them because we thought they would taint us somehow. Instead, these young people walk right into their offices and give them gifts in the spirit of honor and often times they are confused by this honor because they are used to accusation. And the spirit that is functioning in them begins to be disarmed. It is the Kingdom of God coming and these young people have *absolutely* judged that spirit by functioning in the opposing spirit.

That is how you trample serpents and scorpions. You come in the *opposing* spirit as delegates of the higher Authority.

Activation Points:

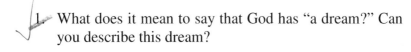

1. What does it mean to say that God has "a dream?" Can you describe this dream?

2. Give an explanation of Galatians 4:1-7. What does this mean?

3. What is a son's or daughter's inheritance?

4. What is the "pre cross commission" and what is the "post cross commission?"

5. Give proof that we have been given "authority" by God to disciple nations.

Spirit of Poverty
Lady Indian lady that had a violent marriage. Started to give her money to pay bills.
Function in the Opposite Spirit.

CHAPTER THREE:

GOD'S DREAM; MY RESPONSIBILITY TO ALL NATIONS

OBSERVE :- notice, perceive something register it as significant / notice, see, perceive / discern detect, spot

If we could encapsulate God's dream in a Scripture, it would be Matthew 28:18

Mission + purpose are interconnected,

Matthew 28:18-20

And Jesus came up and spoke to them, saying, "All authority has been given to Me in Heaven and on earth. Go therefore and make disciples of all the nations, baptizing them in the name of the Father and the Son and the Holy Spirit, teaching them to observe all that I commanded you; and lo, I am with you always, even to the end of the age."

Astronauts -

God has a dream and therefore we have a mission. If He delegated a mission to us, it would be safe to say we have been given authority to fulfill this mission. Within the context of mission is our purpose and destiny. Now, within the context of purpose we are to be reaching souls. Mission and purpose are interconnected. This all sounds very simple and you would think that if anyone on the planet would know to do this it would be Christians. Did you know that some people, who are actually discipling nations (at least through principles) or influencing people, are leaders, such as Oprah, Bono, and other philanthropists like them? Why is it often the rich or wealthy who able to do this? I can tell you it is not because they have money, because I can show you very selfish people who have money and are not doing anything for the poor or needy of the

29

I am blessed so I give back to the community
ABUNDANCE SHIFTS YOU!

world. Rather, philanthropic giving happens **because they realize how blessed they are and that it is a duty for them to give back to the community.** It is because they have at least a glimpse into the Christian principles of love and sowing and reaping and know, at least in some vague sense, that God or good demands that they give to the community. It is sometimes because they simply get to a place where they have so much money and so much wealth that they ask themselves, what is all this for? Their abundance shifts them into thinking they want to give some away. What does that tell you? **Consumption, purely as your reason for being on earth, will never satisfy you.** It is only when you are ready to give away life, which is the exhibition of the nature of God, do you truly begin to feel like you are living. The touch of God is on a person's life when they are giving away. In fact, there is a Jewish psychologist who made a very profound statement when he claimed that 70% of people in mental hospitals might not be there if they functioned and lived by the principle of, "It is more blessed to give than to receive." *It is more blessed to give than receive.*

Science is discovering that when you give and do things for others, it releases a high and a feeling of satisfaction within you. You were meant to give life. So even the unsaved, who maybe have not been redeemed in their spirit-man yet, are actually functioning in God's principles when they are giving away and giving life. We were never meant to be consumers only. The problem often is, when *we become stale* we receive salvation and become immersed in common church culture, our mindsets can still be self-centered. Many come into the house of God as if we have come home to our rich daddy, and we ask Him for more money, for more things, and for more stuff. We are focused on self-consumerism. *Spiritual Consumers* just come to church to get another word from God, and are self-centered. Jesus did not die just so that you could come and attend church. He died for more than that.

Give your life to serve is example of Jesus.

Spiritual Consumers - come for a word
addicted to church.

Giving - changes your body chemistry

For us to live the life of consumers is for us to deny the Gospel at some level. **We read Scripture and know that Jesus and the early church lived a life consumed with the love of God and reaching a lost world.** We know that Jesus had no need of a will because He had no earthly goods to leave to anyone. We know that it cost everything to give your life to Jesus. Yet, we find ourselves coming into a new relationship with the God of the Universe but sometimes still struggle with the spirit of this world which says, "You only live once, get everything you can and hold on to it."

Matthew 8:20

Jesus said to him, "The foxes have holes and the birds of the air have nests, but the Son of Man has nowhere to lay His head."

Multiplication

Jesus was the opposite of a consumer. He multiplied bread and He multiplied fish. Everything Jesus did was multiply life, more life, more healing, and more restoration. In everything He did, He gave away more of Himself, even unto death on a cross. It was for the joy set before Him that He endured and gave away His entire life. Because He gave His life, God the Father said to Him, "Ask of me, and I will give You the nations as Your inheritance." (Psalm 2:8). You see, even for Jesus, destiny was connected to the nations and to people.

Psalm 2:8 (inheritance)

God actually thinks in terms of nations, and why not, He is so big. He is looking down on the planet, and seeing nations as His children. By comparison we are like a speck of dust.

Impact nations

Now, why would God be asking us to go into the world and do something so big? Something that He is actually big enough to do? He has delegated authority to you and He would not tell you to go and do something in which He is not going to back you up. God actually wants to use you to impact nations. Whether that means, your work place, your family, or even by ministering to

31

one person at a time, your faithfulness is impacting nations and even generations.

Take a moment to declare this out loud…

"I have been given authority and have been anointed and have been commissioned to disciple a nation. I accept that, Father, and I am going to get over myself and my selfish desires, the things I think are holding me back, and I just choose right now, to accept that fact. Amen." That is the first step, to accept it. *PRAYer to Disciple a nations*

Now let us break it down further.

What is a Nation? *(marketplace ~ somewhere other than the church)*

The Greek word for nation is *ethnos*. The definition is, "a race, a people group, or a culture group." Perhaps you have heard leaders refer to this term as the *marketplace*. Marketplace is simply anywhere other than the church. Let's make it even more simple. The term marketplace refers to any people group that is outside of the local church. This is the place of harvest, the marketplace. *The place outside the Church is the harvest.*

Here are some examples of nations:

- Canada.
- The education system, schools, these are culture groups (i.e., people groups, which are a type of nation).
- Wal-Mart. Does Wal-Mart have a culture within it? The workers dress the same and have values that the establishment adheres to.
- The justice system.
- Media.
- Daycare centers.
- Government.

- Any workplace. *Every sphere of influence impacted with K.O.G.*

God's dream is to see every sphere of influence impacted with the Kingdom of God. That is why He gave you authority.

How do you disciple a nation? The task of discipling nations definitely takes more than evangelism. It has to be systematic and it has to be broken down into spheres that are manageable. How do you eat an elephant? One bite at a time. How would you ever touch a nation if we as believers remained primarily within the church building, listened to a sermon week after week, and pegged that as the apex of Christianity? How would we ever disciple a nation? So, if God is asking this of us, the church must not just think spiritually, but also strategically. *Church is sub-culture*

Typically, the church has functioned in what is called a *sub-culture*. Meaning we try to influence cultures of the world and nations of the world, while remaining confined to our own spiritual practice within the four walls of the church. That is a sub-culture. Why is it a *sub*? Because we are *under*, which means we are the tail and not the head. At this point in time, we, the church, are meant to be a *counter*-culture. Counter is comprised of against, or an opposing spirit. Consider all the parallels that would comprise us as a counter-culture.

When you function in an opposite spirit, you are functioning from a place of counter-culture. We are to bring *Kingdom* culture. Kingdom culture is a counter-culture to the culture of today. Name a few characteristics that are prevalent of the culture of our day: sexual immorality, humanism, drug abuse, abortion, corruption, hopelessness, suicide, depression, selfishness, lack of self-worth, and divorce, to name a few. This kind of culture of evil actually destroys our societies and deprives nations. Kingdom culture, however, is very much the opposite and has the power to redeem society! **It is the Kingdom of God that has the potential to save society – not the presence of a church building, per se.** If the presence of many church buildings could have affected society, we would have done it by now. There are churches all over the city and all over the world, and the Kingdom of God is within us as individual Christians. But the Kingdom of God, within church members, has not countered the culture of society. We are not giving life to society. We are instead giving individuals church membership. Our society can be changed, however, when believer's are trained and equipped in our churches and sent out to carry the Kingdom into every sphere of life. Some characteristics of Kingdom culture are: love, honesty, honor, mercy, marriage, peace, integrity, blessing, joy, and compassion. It is not that everyone who is unsaved in the world does not function in these. There are many other religions and people groups who function in Kingdom principles, but they do not know Jesus yet. They know SOME Kingdom principles but have not yet met the King of that Kingdom. But *we have a counter-culture.*

We were never meant to be a sub-culture because what we have carries and opposes the fallen culture of the day. So, we were meant to function in the opposite spirit, and that is how we touch nations and people groups, by being a counter-culture to the culture of the day. Going boldly into society, carrying the spirit of grace, and the principles of the Kingdom of God, we were never meant to run and hide.

We must realize that the end goal is not to restrict ourselves within a sub-culture. Remember, Adam and Eve were created in the image of God and placed in the Garden of Eden where they had complete dominion over everything in the earth. They were not the sub-culture. Neither were they the counter-culture. They were THE culture!

First Step

The first step in our journey (the Great Commission) is to become the catalysts of a counter-culture.

Level of Influence
The Gates Must Be Taken.

This is the level of influence the church was created to have. She had this level of influence in the Roman Empire in the 300s. She was not able to maintain the influence. We must learn from the history of the church. Learn how to become the counter-culture and ultimately, THE culture. We must learn how to maintain that level of influence without falling prey to the temptations that often caused the church in the centuries after Christ to lose her influence on the culture. *King rules over the spheres.*

In each of the seven sociological spheres, the Kingdom of God is to have rulership. The world knows that whoever governs that sphere of life and rules that sphere of life, has rulership. There was a time when a group of Christian leaders sat on a certain board, and for Hollywood to be able to release a movie, it had to be approved by a board of Christian leaders. Do you know what happened to that board? Those Christian leaders said in essence, "We do not want to do this anymore because the kingdom of Hollywood is secular. It is not our place to control this kingdom. We should be concerned with what is happening in the churches." They gave back their influence and retreated into the church. When one kingdom leaves, another kingdom rushes in. So the kingdom of darkness capitalized on this and took over that kingdom, because whoever has the gate, has the authority. The gates must be taken.

The Seven Spheres of Society

1. Family – Do we have a need for a ministry to families? We are seeing the kingdom of darkness taking authority over our families. This is happening within the church and not just out in the world. People are coming to church and still getting divorced. It is the Kingdom of God, the counter-culture within *you* that is able to restore families, and thus become the culture.

2. Church or religion – Does the Kingdom of God need to be in the church? I have been to some churches and asked, "Where is the Kingdom of God? Where is the

35

love? Where is the anointing?" The kingdom of God needs to penetrate the Church.

3. Education system – Do we need a counter-culture to come and permeate the education system? Absolutely, we need people to get into this system and bring Kingdom principles to reform it.

4. Government – We need a counter-culture. We need the Kingdom of Heaven to invade government.

5. Business – We need honest practices, quality products, genuine, authentic business leaders who understand the principles of the Kingdom of God and apply them to their work life. Good business practices. We need a counter-culture and *we* carry it! You have it! We are supposed to be bringing that there.

6. Media – Can you imagine if Christian leaders possessed the gates of media or even influenced media on a greater scale? We have settled for too little for too long!

7. Arts and entertainment – We have the same spirit that raised Jesus from the dead inside of us. This is the Spirit of the One Who created the Universe. We should be the most creative and artistic people on the planet. We must no longer be content to work at the arts in a way that produces mediocre products and set present mediocre standards for what is art and entertainment.

So understand that the world breaks it down this way, and we do too. There are nations within these spheres of influence.

Do you know to what category you are called? Maybe you are not in it yet, but you know you are called to it.

That is the kind of cultural revolution we are going to become! Imagine a world where the Kingdom of God has come to the earth as it exists in Heaven.

Counter-Culture
- a way of life - set of attitudes opposed to the social norm (status quo)

Activation Points:

1. List each of the seven mountains/spheres, and for each one, list five aspects of the worldly culture of the day. Then, list five of the opposites, which are Kingdom culture.

2. Example: For the Kingdom culture or sphere of **family**, one worldly culture/opposite would be divorce. So the opposite of divorce would be marriage. So you are listing 5 prevalent worldly kingdom cultures and you are listing the five Kingdom opposites.

3. Then underneath each one I want you to list a dream or a brainstorm of what kind of ministry God could give you to meet those issues; write a brief paragraph. What would it look like? What does it look like to minister to families? If you could have your dream, like a TV show or something that targets your family, what would it be? List an example of a ministry that targets each of those issues; one ministry for each sphere. If money were not an issue and you could have that ministry, what would it be, what would it look like for each? The paragraph should be a description of the ministry. You do not need to have the Scripture reference for the Biblical principle, but a Biblical principle should be the foundation of the opposing culture. So, do not just say drug addiction and then say counselling, go deeper and answer what kind of counselling. Discuss the ministry in detail. What are you countering that culture with? What are you bringing to the table?

CHAPTER FOUR:

WHEN GOD PUTS YOU IN YOUR PLACE

Everyone in life has been given a place to occupy; a domain. You are called by God for a purpose. Everyone, even the man who is locked up in prison, who committed a crime, still has a purpose and is called to occupy. He may not be occupying his place right now because of sin, or ignorance but he is still called. **Every person in life is called to do something, to lead and to be excellent in some way.** The very reason that we have, within our nature a feeling of purpose, denotes this fact.

The Bible says, "Without vision the people perish" (Proverbs 29:18), and so when you see people who have no idea what their purpose is, examine closely how they carry themselves. Perhaps they are living a negative lifestyle or hurting themselves; they do this because they do not have a vision of what their purpose is. Everyone is looking for his or her purpose. Most people know they have a purpose in something, but they do not know how to find it and so they settle for the enemy's purpose. Just as much as God has a purpose for your life, so does the devil and so many people are walking in the will of Satan. We see very clearly that there is a need for the people of God to take up their place on this earth.

We know, from the shape the world is in, that there is a great need for you to step up into your sphere of influence and start making a difference. Creation groans for the revealing of the sons of God. You are needed, now, like never before. The more chaos the earth is in, the more evident it is that we need to step into our God-given talents and gifts and do the work He called us to do.

This is not the time to shrink back. This is the time to press forward with a fierceness that comes from knowing who we are in Christ. This is the time for fierceness that comes from knowing what He has called us to. That fierceness comes from walking in the anointed place where we are in the perfect center of God's will for our lives.

Matthew 20:20-22

Then the mother of the sons of Zebedee came to Jesus with her sons, bowing down and making a request of Him. And He said to her, "What do you wish?" She said to Him, "Command that in Your kingdom these two sons of mine may sit one on Your right and one on Your left." But Jesus answered, "You do not know what you are asking. Are you able to drink the cup that I am about to drink?"

What Jesus is saying here is that not even He prepares your place in life. There is a place that God, the Father, has fixed for you to do, even while you were in your mother's womb. He has prepared a place for you that no other can fulfill. These two sons of Zebedee, James and John, actually watched as their mother made a request of Jesus about their places. She asked Jesus if they could sit on Jesus' right and left. Now let's understand that to have a desire such as this is not wrong. Their desire was right, but their method was wrong. You can pray all you want for a place or position in life, but God may never give it to you because He has a place already prepared for you. Jesus said, "This is not Mine to give, only God knows whether you are able to occupy this place, this domain," and that is the same today for every person.

God has fixed, by His authority, a place, or a promised land for you to conquer and reap the benefits thereof. Every person was born to excel and rule in their place of calling.

Every person was born with certain gifts and anointing. Your gifts, talents, and abilities are keys to you becoming great in your domain or place of purpose. For example: I was in Alabama once and went to the Shakespeare Music Festival where I saw a lady play the piano like I could never imagine. She was unbelievable. And I looked at her and thought, "That woman has been born with a gift." Her gift was a clue to what her purpose was – and she had definitely discovered it. There was evidence that revealed what she was called to do. Your giftings are keys to your greatness in that area to which God has called you. Every person has been given a gift or gifts. You have to ask yourself what your gifts are, because your gifts "make room for you." (Proverbs 18:16). This means that if you cultivate that gifting that God has given you, that gift will cause you to rise to platforms of influence. Proverbs also says that a man who excels in his work will stand before kings (Proverbs 22:29).

Gifting is natural - full of peace!

It is important to understand that when you find your place of gifting it will be a place that is natural for you. This does not mean that it will not take a lot of work or an incredible amount of study to get there and maintain your place. It merely means that it will be a place of peace. Even in the face of great turmoil, you will find yourself at peace. Even when everything around is falling apart and people are in a panic, you will find yourself at peace, able to function.

There is also a steadiness that only comes from being in the place where God has called and gifted you. The opposite is also true. If you are outside your area of calling or gifting, you will find that nothing can bring peace. Even when everything is calm, you will find yourself in turmoil. Even when you have what many would define as prosperity, you will find yourself discontented. It is impossible to run from the calling of God and find peace. It is impossible to work outside your area of gifting and be as effective as when you are in your area of calling.

We spend too little time trying to discern what our gifts and callings are. We spend too little time working in the area of our calling. As a result, we too often find ourselves completely ineffective in anything we do – even when it is good ministry work. For example, even though it is a good thing to travel to a foreign country and preach the Gospel or work on the streets, if you are called to work with young people in the inner city, your greatest area of effectiveness will be in the inner city working with youth. This does not mean that you should not go on the mission trip to some far away country. Your gifts and abilities are connected to your calling, and your calling is connected to somewhere specifically. God is a master strategist.

It is also important for us to define prosperity because, often in the West, we have a very warped view of what prosperity is. There is a great temptation to define success as a big house, a large piece of land or a beach home, a luxury car, and all of our debt paid off. While that is a form of prosperity, it is not how God defines prosperity.

Matthew 16:24-26

Then Jesus said to His disciples, "If anyone wishes to come after Me, he must deny himself, and take up his cross and follow Me. For whoever wishes to save his life will lose it; but whoever loses his life for My sake will find it. For what will it profit a man if he gains the whole world and forfeits his soul? Or what will a man give in exchange for his soul?

From this passage we can clearly see that it is possible to "gain the world" or to have even a measure of worldly success but lose our soul. I think this Scripture also reveals that there is much we can do and give ourselves to on this earth that is really only vanity – vanity that has no real eternal goal or significance.

We often have a very narrow view of success. Part of the reason for this is we do not live with eternity in mind. We get bogged down in the worries of this life and forget that most of our existence will be spent living in eternity. The house we are struggling to buy will eventually turn to dust. We will die and the work that we believe we are critical to will continue on most likely without a moment's hesitation.

We do not understand what King David declared when he announced that life is a mere breath (Psalm 39:5). If we could find a way to always live with eternity in mind, we would have less trouble defining prosperity from a Biblical perspective. **Prosperity from God's view point is always about living in such a way that we are storing up treasures in Heaven rather than on the earth.**

With true prosperity comes fulfillment, joy, and peace.

Working a job or having a career (unless it is your purpose) will never bring you genuine prosperity, fulfillment, joy, or peace. These fruits are byproducts of living in your purpose. This is not saying that you should NOT work, for Scripture says, "If anyone is not willing to work, then he is not to eat, either." (2 Thessalonians 3:10). You will not find all of those blessings in your work unless you are totally in your purpose. Now that I have found my purpose, the sense of joy that I have is so deep. My purpose has brought me joy; my purpose has brought me freedom and happiness; my purpose has brought me financial blessing; my purpose has taken me all over the world. Walking out my purpose supplies my needs and it is a blessing to me.

Your number one pursuit in life, other than Jesus, is to discover your place and purpose. If you want to discover your place and purpose, get in touch with God and He will move mountains to get you there. Sometimes I have trouble relating to people who come to me and do not know their place or purpose. The reason being, because when I made it my number one pursuit to be like Jesus, He naturally whipped open doors for me. Suddenly I was in my place, and before long I understood that God was my manager. So if you are wondering what your place is, you need to have a Moses' burning bush experience. You need to seek the face of God until He calls you clearly into your purpose. This might not happen quickly, and there may even be a painful process involved. In Moses' case he was just doing what he was doing on a regular basis. One day he encountered a burning bush where God spoke to him and told him that his purpose was to lead all of Israel out of bondage (Exodus 3). You must find out the place God has reserved for you, because the place you are chasing may not be as good as the place He has chosen for you.

It is important to discover your purpose and cultivate your own garden. **When you discover your place in life, it does not drain you of life, instead it gives you life and empowers you.** Doing what you are called to do empowers you; it is the reason you get up in the morning; it is the reason you fast; it is the reason you praise; it is the reason you have joy! But you must cultivate your relationship with God, and your own development. you must pray into your purpose, you must prepare for it, and you must focus on your vision. You have joy and you become a person who is alive, you become a person who is living! It is a shame that many unsaved people come across as if they are more alive than Christians. Famous celebrities like Brad Pitt and Angelina Jolie are changing the world and adopting orphans, doing exactly what the Bible says to do, and are praised for all the good they are doing.

Instead of judging them for not being Christians, we should be learning from them. They are managing, at least in this one area of their lives, to live the Kingdom lifestyle, without the benefit of knowing Jesus. There is a lesson here for us. We must do what He commands, when it is easy, and when it is hard. We are bought with a price and our lives are not our own. How can we allow others, who are not sold out to the Gospel, to live better Christian lives than we are living?

For too long we have believed that only those in full-time classical ministry were living called lives. We must learn that each of us are called to live a life of full-time ministry, no matter where we work. If we do what God created us to do it will be a job of full-time ministry. It will be a job that changes the world just as much as the life and ministry of a full-time evangelist or pastor.

Nine Keys to Discovering Your Place or Purpose:

I would like to credit Myles Monroe whose life and ministry inspired some of these keys. Dr. Monroe's commitment to the Lordship of Jesus influenced people all over the world, including me.

You need to answer the following questions:

1. What is my deepest desire? *Help WomEN/SupPRessioN*
2. What is my deepest passion? If the devil cannot take your salvation, he will get you working in the wrong garden. No one else can fill that place that you have been called to.
3. What makes me angry? You were born to solve a problem. *iNjustice to womeN.*
4. What ideas are persistent? *WomEN*
5. What do I constantly imagine? Imagination is often your purpose in pictures. Take inventory about what you think about.
6. What do I wish I could do for humanity? When you are determining your purpose always try to think of others, not just yourself.
7. What are my reoccurring dreams?
8. What brings me the greatest fulfillment? Do not just do what you are told to do, do not just do what you have to

do, ask yourself what really brings you fulfillment and do everything you can to begin to do that, at any cost.

9. What would I do for no money? The secret is that God funds the vision when you work for the government of God!

What would I rather be doing than what I am currently doing now?

Answering these questions will help each of us better understand what gifts and talents God has placed in our souls. Very few of us live a life of self-evaluation to the level that we are already well prepared to understand how God made us and what makes us tick.

Few people ever get beyond the place of living from day-to-day, trying to merely get by. They spend their time letting life decide how they are going to live instead of deciding how they are going to live their own lives. There is a subtle difference between these two approaches to life, but if we can master this one concept we can become more effective for God every day.

By taking the time to answer these questions you will actually be taking steps to better determine how God made you. You will be positioned like few people on the face of the earth. It will give you a leg up on the people around you who might be living for God, they might be doing everything they know to fulfill His calling on their life. It is harder for them, however, because they have never taken the time to determine what their gifts are. They do not truly know what God has called them to do.

Very few people search for their calling and their gifting in a radical way. Even fewer Christians take the time to find their calling or their gifting. The time is getting shorter. The workers are few (Mathew 9:37). It is critical that we get out into the spheres of influence where God has called us and gifted us.

Activation Points:

1. What is my deepest desire? What is my deepest passion?

2. What makes me angry? What problem would I like to solve for humanity?

3. What ideas and dreams are persistent in my life?

4. What brings me the greatest fulfillment? Do not just do what you are told to do, do not just do what you have to do, ask yourself what really brings you fulfillment and do everything you can to begin to do that, at any cost.

5. What would I do even if I was not paid for it?

CHAPTER FIVE:

PURSUING YOUR PROMISED LAND

What is the Promised Land? Biblically and geographically the Promised Land was a physical place flowing with milk and honey. It was the place that the Israelites were to occupy, the place that God had already given them and they were to take and conquer (Leviticus 20:24). It was destined to be their domain. We see a type of this when we look at the Garden of Eden.

What are the two roles of man on the earth?

1. Relationship with God.
2. To work in the Garden; to work the land where God placed Adam.

Genesis 1:28

God blessed them; and God said to them, "Be fruitful and multiply, and fill the earth, and subdue it; and rule over the fish of the sea and over the birds of the sky and over every living thing that moves on the earth."

In other words, God told us to take dominion and to take rulership. **God has blessed us to rule and have dominion, managing the area that God has placed us.**

Principle #1

God does not bless you just for your own benefit. The reason He blessed them was so they could be a blessing to others. God blessed them to be "fruitful, multiply, to fill the earth, and subdue it." Whenever God blesses you in some way it is not just for you to enjoy, it is so that someone else can be blessed through you. God uses His church that way!

Principle #2

God told them to be fruitful, to multiply and to fill the earth, and subdue it. God told the first man and the first woman to subdue the earth. Because they failed, and because of sin, they lost the glory and the ability to truly bring Kingdom influence on earth. Jesus, however, came and taught us how to do just that. So the principle, according to Genesis 1:28, is that *it is in your very nature to desire Godly dominion and the establishment of God's Kingdom on earth.* This means it should be in your nature to be a catalyst of change in your world where God has placed you.

You were born to have rulership and excel in your purpose or promised land. You were born to use your gifts and talents to bring the kingdom of Heaven to earth within your sphere of influence. Make no mistake about it, everybody has a sphere of influence. Every one of us has someone who looks to us for direction and God wants to use all of us to bring the Kingdom of God to the earth. We are all leaders in some respect – whether it is leadership over a country, a state, a city, a village, a street, a block, a home, or even over one life.

Genesis 2:7-8,15

Then the Lord God formed man of dust from the ground, and breathed into his nostrils the breath of life; and man became a living being. The Lord God planted a garden toward the east, in Eden; and there He placed the man whom He had formed....

Then the Lord God took the man and put him into the garden of Eden to cultivate it and keep it.

I am called to cultivate a garden. You are called to cultivate a garden. This garden is a type or a picture of a promised land, a place flowing with good things, a place that we are to establish His Kingdom in. Your promised land is your sphere of influence.

It is never too late to find your sphere of influence. It is never too late to start cultivating your garden. It is critical to God's plan that you find your place and begin influencing it to fulfill God's dream.

Principle #3

Every person has been given a garden or promised land in which to be faithful. It does not matter who you are, it does not matter whether you know what that particular place is. There has been a promised land prepared for you to manage and rule well!

One thing is certain, **God has given you gifts and talents that are unique to you.** He has called you to serve Him using your gifts and talents. He expects this much from each of us. He will give you wisdom as to how best to use your gifts and talents. He will guide you by His Spirit.

At the end of the day, however, He expects you to show some initiative and actually exercise your gifts and talents. Then, He will bless your efforts and bring change to the sphere of influence where you are called.

Principle #4

Your promised land requires your effort and work. From it comes rewards and blessing and new life. You were meant to be rewarded by the fruitfulness of the garden and from your promised land. Your life can become a great adventure, your life can become so full of joy that the heathen looks at you and asks, "Why are you still blessed?" And you would reply with, "God has blessed me because I have discovered my place of promise and from my place of promise comes my reward." You were not born in vain; God did not save you in vain; you were not delivered in vain; you were placed on earth for a purpose, to occupy and establish the Kingdom of God in your promised land.

Nothing in life comes without effort. Part of the very nature of the Universe is what you sow you reap. If you do not work, you do not eat (2 Thessalonians 3:10). These laws are God's way of ensuring that we are doing what He has called us to do.

There is something incredibly rewarding about working, in your sphere of calling, putting in your time, and then seeing the results of your hard work come to fruition. There is something terribly justifying in seeing someone fail to put the work in and not getting out what they had expected. That is because we all inherently understand that it takes effort to produce something worthwhile in this world. Our garden was created to be fertile. It was also created in such a way that fertility is only possible when you do your part to see everything through to the harvest.

Exodus 1:22

Then Pharaoh commanded all his people, saying, "Every son who is born you are to cast into the Nile, and every daughter you are to keep alive."

Principle #5

If the devil cannot steal your salvation, he will try to keep you from your destiny. I fear that many in the Body of Christ today are not doing much with their salvation. The devil has been able to keep us in the church pew to such an extent we have not been able to embrace our own purpose and place of calling. Therefore, we have not realized our full potential as deliverers, we have just become safe and even passive.

The devil is working daily, maybe not to take away your salvation but to keep you from becoming who you were born to be, to keep you from becoming a deliverer. He does it through sin; he does it through distractions; and most of all, he does it through laziness. You finding your promised land means other people's deliverance! The devil cannot let you come into your place of power; he cannot let you come into rulership over your garden because if you do, you will set captives free. He tried the same with Jesus. What happened when Jesus was to be born? The king ordered all the male children under two years of age to be murdered (Mathew 2:16), it was another abortion-like scenario to try and stop this deliverer from being raised up. The devil does not want you coming into your destiny because it means the deliverance of many others. Now, this of course did not work with Moses because we know that Moses' mother took him and placed him in a basket and placed it in the river. Then Pharaoh's daughter came to the river and found him and decided to keep him.

Exodus 2:10

The child grew, and she brought him to Pharaoh's daughter and he became her son. And she named him Moses, and said, "Because I drew him out of the water."

What a miracle! Pharaoh is trying to kill this leader and his daughter becomes the mother of the child that is going to deliver all of Israel. This is the irony of God.

One of the most fulfilling things in life is surviving hard times to get to the Promised Land. It is only after wandering in the wilderness for 40 years (Numbers 32:13), that we can truly appreciate the goodness of the Promised Land. It is the hard work that leads to the reward that helps us better relish living in the law of God's promise. Without the hard work we would be more likely to take the graciousness of God for granted.

Principle #6

God will often prepare you to receive your promise in unlikely, challenging, and difficult places. You must understand the seasons of life. Sometimes we underestimate where we are going because we are not recognizing where we are.

Here, Moses is about to be trained in the very place from which he is going to deliver and set people free. There are times in your life where you find yourself in the very opposite of your place of calling. You do not know why you are there; you do not know what you are going to do there; but for some reason God has placed you there. If you despise that place despite how painful it may feel you might just miss a crucial training ground necessary for you to become a deliverer in your world. Moses is growing up in Pharaoh's palace and is learning the ways of Egypt. Later in his life we read in Exodus that he stumbles upon an Egyptian beating and hurting a Hebrew and something rises up within Moses. Moses killed the Egyptian and word begins to spread and Pharaoh finds out (Exodus 2:11-15). The Bible says even though Moses was like a son to Pharaoh, Pharaoh now is going to kill Moses for killing the Egyptian. The very place that Moses was being trained, he was then being chased out of.

Exodus 2:15

When Pharaoh heard of this matter, he tried to kill Moses. But Moses fled from the presence of Pharaoh and settled in the land of Midian, and he sat down by a well.

Did Moses do wrong and sin in killing the Egyptian? Yes, that was wrong, it was not God who made him do that. Moses sinned but God can work all things together for good (Romans 8:28). God is never put off by our sin. In fact, He has a cure for every sin we have ever committed or ever will commit.

God's promises often come in the least expected way. There are many times when we get to the end of the road and realize that it happened completely differently than we would have expected. It is often that it happens differently than we could have imagined. God works in such a way that we have to rely on Him rather than merely relying on a formula for going forward. This is part of the beauty of finding out where God has called you and working in your sphere of influence. It is always exciting to see how God is working in any given situation.

Principle #7

Your past mistakes do not necessarily hinder you from your Promised Land. God can work all things together for good. It does not matter if you were a criminal who spent time in prison; God always has a way of bringing things around for His glory.

It does not matter what your past looks like, God has a way of fulfilling your future and bringing you into promise. The promises He gave you are still applicable; you can still seize them. In Exodus 2:15, we read that when Pharaoh heard of this matter he tried to kill Moses, so Moses fled. He then settled in the land of Midian and he sat down by a well and his heart was being developed. Have you ever felt like you have been sitting in the desert, asking yourself, "Where am I going or, what am I doing?"

No matter where you are currently placed, even though it might not be your promised land, be a faithful servant! Moses served those people whom he did not even know. If you can be a servant in the place you despise, you can be a servant and rule in your sphere of influence. Serving is key to your promotion. Serve in that place, whether you like it or not, and you will become greater. If God knows that you can serve in the menial things, He will have you serve the world through something great. Many of us have not been able to serve in the great capacities or rule in the Promised Land yet because we have not served in the desert. If you can serve when you feel lost, if you have the kind of heart that God can trust you to serve those around you when things are not going well, He will raise you up to serve in a greater capacity.

Serving is key to your promotion. Can you serve from the heart? Can you do a menial task for a long period of time? If you read about the life of Moses, he spent a long time in Midian. There are people in the Bible who waited 40 years before their destiny opened up. Moses was one of those people. Serving is key to your promotion!

God is the great redeemer. He does not see you as you are. Rather, He sees you as He created you to be, complete with your gifts and callings. He knows who you are created to be. He knows what you are capable of doing. He is patient and willing to give you time to come into your calling. He is faithful to give you what you need to get to the place of grace where you are influencing those who are in your sphere of influence.

Exodus 2:21

Moses was willing to dwell with the man, and he gave his daughter Zipporah to Moses.

Principle #8

Though you are not yet in your promised land, be content with where God has placed you for now. God might be testing your heart. Moses was living lavishly in the palace with Pharaoh and he lost everything. He was far from the palace, but he was closer to his Promised Land than ever.

I choose to look at every season of my life as though I will never go beyond. So for example, when I did just youth ministry, I treated my youth ministry as though I would never do anything else and I put all my energy into being the best youth pastor possible. You have to take your Promised Land and make it into your platform for the world to see you. We are here to take what we think is menial and do such a good job at it that we become famous, that the whole world is talking about you! Faithfulness is doing it with all your might and from your heart, in the area God has given you.

God often keeps us where we are to help us mature into where we are going. It is important to learn to be comfortable with where we are, maintaining hope and faith for something greater later. But He has something for us today! Right where we are. Something that might well determine where we end up. The best way to get to the next phase in our life is to be faithful in this phase of our life. When we are faithful with what is put before us we are better able to grow into the fullness of our gifts and talents.

Exodus 2:23

Now it came about in the course of those many days that the king of Egypt died. And the sons of Israel sighed because of the bondage, and they cried out; and their cry for help because of their bondage rose up to God.

Principle #9

Do not be anxious about finding your place. The stages and seasons of your life are often limited to time. Everything God does is within time. It does not matter where you go in the world, it takes nine months to give birth to a baby. In Amsterdam it takes women nine months as well as in Canada. Everything is limited by time.

Much like principle #8, this principle requires us to be content where we are, while at the same time longing to be where He has called us to be. It is in this place of contentment that we find out what we are really made of. It is here that we learn how much God has done for us. It is here that we get the vision for where He has called us.

Timing is the hardest thing to learn. It is hard to learn when to stay still, when to move forward, when to speak, and when to be silent. These lessons are critical for us to walk into the maturity that comes from being a Son of God. This is the place where our greatest gifts and talents come to bear.

Moses could have tried all he wanted to go back and save Israel, but if it was not God's timing, he would have failed. He could have been doing the very thing God called him to, but failed, because it was not the right time. The stages of your life are limited by time. You need to recognize that God can be putting you in a season of time where prayer and preparation is required for you to step into your destiny.

Every one of us has an appointed time of release and when you allow time to lead you into your place of promise, God's grace will be upon you. What you did not do well before, you will suddenly be able to do because it is the right time.

You can go from the desert to kingly rulers in a heartbeat. God is able to promote you and raise you up so fast that your head will spin, but He is more concerned about where your heart is. Your character has to be ready to handle that next level. God is not about you receiving your title, He wants you to prosper. He wants to give you success in your area of influence. He must, however, deal with character or your promised land will destroy you.

Surrender to the process – surrender to what God wants to deal with in you, before you are promoted to the next level and before you take your promised land. I allow God to do this in me, because the deeper you push me into the earth, the greater my resurrection will be. Moses became great and the Bible says he was the humblest man in the world (Numbers 12:3). He led the Israelites and became the greatest prophet; he was a man that the Bible says God spoke with face to face (Deuteronomy 34:10).

Start by putting some legs to that Scripture. You do not need more deliverance; it is your habits that need to change. Old habits need to be replaced by new ones. Your life will become a mystery to people. If God can trust you with small, then He will give you great and He will exalt you. Not for your own gain, but so that others can be led out of bondage. So, take your scars, take your pains, and the struggles you currently have, and say, "Lord let this be a suffering that saves somebody someday. Let it be a suffering that makes me worthy of my promised land."

The world is waiting for you. There are people who will not see Heaven unless you possess your place of promise. No matter what the cost, stop living for yourself and live with others in mind. Every time I feel like I do not want to pray and fast or surrender to the process, I think of all the people that need to be reached and I remember it is worth it. Your church membership will not deliver anybody; your level of set-apartness, of holiness, and friendship with God can deliver a nation.

Why is it important to serve faithfully in your current location? Why is it important to give your all, if it is your promise?

The Bible is clear that those who are faithful in little will be trusted with greater things (Luke 16:10). Faithfulness is a gift that we grow into. It is not a gift that we inherently understand.

It takes practice. It takes working through little temptations to walk away from your place to get to the place where we are willing to stand – no matter what the cost.

It is also important that you give your all. Remember that Jesus gave everything to bring you into right relationship with God. Why would you do anything less than everything we can in exchange for such a great sacrifice? The only way to be faithful in the small things is to give your all at whatever you are doing. You cannot be faithful if you are not giving your all at every moment. Though giving your all is not required to gain your promise, giving your all is required to show yourself faithful.

Faithfulness brings you into your promised land. Faithfulness brings you to the place of honor in the Kingdom of God. Once you have proven faithful in any matter God is better able to continue giving to you.

Faithfulness and hard work are also important to show that you can be trusted with the blessings of God. God does not want to give you something that will destroy you. So, He gives you a little and checks to see your demeanor. The next time He gives you a little more. And He continues as you show yourself faithful.

God will often prepare you to receive your promised land in unlikely, challenging, and difficult places. Why does God allow you to go through challenging and wilderness seasons, when He can just give you your promised land now?

Through difficulties we learn to walk in the spirit and not by sight or in the flesh. God wants to teach us when difficult times occur. At those times we connect with Him in a greater and more intimate way and it is in the difficult times that our faith is strengthened and perfected as gold.

It is in difficult times that we are refined. Often we learn more from lack and from struggle than we do from blessings. It is part of the nature of fallen man that we stumble in the good times and yet become closer to God and His Kingdom during times of struggle.

Exodus 3:1-3

Now Moses was pasturing the flock of Jethro his father-in-law, the priest of Midian; and he led the flock to the west side of the wilderness and came to Horeb, the mountain of God. The angel of the Lord appeared to him in a blazing fire from the midst of a bush; and he looked, and behold, the bush was burning with fire, yet the bush was not consumed. So Moses said, "I must turn aside now and see this marvelous sight, why the bush is not burned up.

Here we see that Moses is a shepherd and at this point he has gone from a high place in his life to a very low place. It seems like he has gone in the opposite direction of his call. He was a prince in the very palaces of Egypt, where the highest-ranking person you could be under was Pharaoh. He is now exiled, shepherding with Jethro, and it looks as though he is going to be a shepherd for the rest of his life. God sees the big picture! Moses did not know what was about to happen to him as he served faithfully in the field, knowing not whether he would ever be more than what he currently was. Then God interrupted his life with a fiery burning bush out of which God Himself spoke.

Moses' training in faithfulness did not end with the voice of God from the burning bush. His training continued being faithful in the small things in order to be moved to the big things. Even at this point in his life Moses did not believe he was the right person for the task God had prepared. This is an important point. Moses was incredibly humble.

Imagine, you are the person called to lead the children of Israel out of over 400 years of slavery in Egypt and yet, in spite of that calling, you still believe that God has chosen the wrong person. You cannot fake that level of humility. That is why it is important to be faithful in little things. It teaches us that God is the one who brings increase. It teaches us that there should be absolutely no pride in fulfilling our calling.

It really helps us remember that it is God who is working, when we never lose sight of the fact that God chose to speak through a donkey. If He can use a donkey (Numbers 22:28), He can use you and me. If He can use a donkey, we should not be puffed up with pride when He chooses to use us.

I believe that not every person actually enters into his or her promised land. It is a great tragedy that some people live 80-90 years of their life making money, eating, sleeping, making more money, and then dying, having never walked into their promise.

What is your promised land? It is your place of calling, a place to which God has called you. It is the place where, once you step into it, you say, "This is what I was born to do!"

Here, in Exodus 3:1, we see Moses was pastoring the flock of Jethro, his father-in-law, and he came to the mountain of God where the angel of the Lord appeared to him in a blazing fire, from the midst of a bush. He looked and behold the bush was burning with fire.

Principle #10

When God says it's time, He will interrupt you where you are currently serving. If you are serving faithfully where God has placed you, there will come a time where, after you have been faithful, He actually interrupts you and promotes you. When this happens, no man can stop it. In fact, you cannot even stop it, unless you decide to rebel against it.

There is no stopping it when that door opens and God says it is time. If you are faithful where you are currently planted, when God says it is time, He will interrupt your life. He will push negative things aside, He will open doors that no man can open or shut, and He will put you in your place. You will be seen by the world as a son or daughter of Heaven.

When God says it is time, He will interrupt you where you are currently serving. So, Moses said, "I must turn aside now and see this marvelous sight." Notice the Holy Spirit's wording here. It is not an accident that Moses says, "I must turn aside and pay attention to what is happening; here is something that I need to give my attention to. I must pay attention to what God might be saying to me." The Scripture actually says in verse 4, that when the Lord saw that he turned aside and looked, God called to him. There comes a point in your life and your destiny when God will not play hard to get. He will throw out an opportunity to you and He will see if you are paying attention and are staying in tune with His Spirit.

King David was shepherding his father's flock while his brothers were out fighting the King's battles. He was defending his charges, the sheep of his father, against the bear and lion when no one was watching (1 Samuel 17:34). He was being faithful in small things. Not thinking about preparing for greater things, but doing what he had been called to do at that moment in time.

David's faithfulness made him the prime candidate for moving forward with God. Without questioning God, David was doing what he had been told to do. Therefore, God was able to promote him.

Remember, David's promotion to king, however, was not overnight. David spent a long time living with the promise of being the king without actually being the king. He had to be faithful, even in the light of the promise for a long time – before he saw the promise fulfilled. All those nights hiding in the caves prepared David to be a better king. All of those days fearing for his life left David better prepared to serve the people of Israel in righteousness. All those days of struggle helped David become a man after God's own heart! What greater testimony could there be given of any of us?

Principle #11

You *must* be alert for the sign of God's calling. There is a divine tension involved when it comes to destiny. Yes, God does the work for us, but at the same time He wants us to be alert and have our spiritual eyes and ears tuned to what He is saying.

In short, you have got to get up in the morning and read your Bible and pray, because if you never speak to God, you will not recognize His voice or His words. We have to know His voice for us to understand when to go left once you go right or when to move here or move there. We have to know His voice for us to know what school to go to, who to marry, and these important destiny questions that we have. We must practice hearing and see that we have to be a friend of God, so that when we see a bush that is burning, we know it is Him trying to get our attention.

Now, these bushes could easily have caught fire because of how dry it was. Moses could have passed by that bush thinking that it was a regular brushfire, but he did not. He stopped and had the insight to realize he needed to recognize that something was different about this bush. He probably wondered if someone was trying to tell him something. Then he realized the bush was speaking to him, and as Moses approaches the voice, God's very invitation was that Moses remove his sandals because he was standing on holy ground. You can never approach God and step into your destiny until He has purified you and prepared you properly.

There are so many ways to fail, that it is important for us to walk in purity of thought and action. That is why Jesus talked about lust in your heart being the same as adultery (Mathew 5:28). He knew that everything happens in the heart. Out of the abundance of the heart the mouth speaks. If you do not take the time to purify your heart, you will find yourself incapable of fulfilling God's purpose in your life.

On the other hand, if you have a pure heart, you will find yourself much better prepared to move forward with all that God has for you. If you can walk in purity, then God can trust you to do what is right and honorable for those you are serving. This is the place that is occupied by sons and daughters.

Principle #12

Without holiness you will only corrupt your promised land or be further corrupted by the evils you were meant to subdue there! **Your devotional life and practice of the Presence of Jesus purifies you and prepares you for your promised land.** God told Moses to take off his shoes (Exodus 3:5). You need shoes to walk in the desert! God was saying to him that not only was it a holiness lesson, but it was also that He was going to give Moses new shoes designed for the walk that was coming. God said, "I'm giving you a new walk of life."

God also said, "I am the God of your father, the God of Abraham, the God of Isaac, and the God of Jacob." (Exodus 3:6). It is important to know why God does not just say here, "I am God." God was basically giving Moses a little illustration of the fact that He made a covenant with Abraham and He kept it with

Isaac his son and He made a covenant promise and kept it with Jacob. What God was saying to Moses is, "What I am about to do is so great, and you need to know that I am a promise keeping God and if I say I called you to do this thing, then I really have." No matter how intimidating your promised land is, God promises to be your protection.

This is critical because it is often difficult getting out of the desert into your promised land. God has a way of taking you through all the processes necessary to be truly prepared to rule in the sphere of influence which is your promised land. That is why you need to know what your calling is. That is why you need to be pure. That is why you need to be humble. Without everything working in the right order it is impossible to accomplish all God has for you.

Just as He did for Moses, God wants to accomplish for you what He accomplished for Abraham, Isaac, and Jacob. God wants to accomplish something that will have significance now. He wants to accomplish something that will have generational significance. He wants to change the part of the world over which you have influence through your life and your ministry. This is huge!

Principle #13

God is not giving you your promised land only for your benefit; He has others in mind! God said to Moses, "The cry of My people has come to Me and it is time to set them free. Therefore, I am sending you!" (Exodus 3:9-10). What happened with Moses? He was minding his own business, just shepherding in the field, and he had an encounter with God.

You must understand that you are called to a life of service to others. Your life, when lived only for your own benefit, consumes and destroys you. It is only as you learn to lay down your life for the sake of those around you that you can truly live a life that is what God created you to live. That is the place of greatest fulfillment. That is the place of greatest peace.

Like Jesus, you must learn to answer the call of God, even when it does not appear to be in your best interest. You must learn to work and live in our sweet spot. At the same time, you have to live a life completely surrendered to His will if we want to reach the place of greatness to which He has called you and created you to reach.

Then, like Jesus, you will be involved in something so much bigger than yourself that we will see the world transformed. We will see the Kingdom of Heaven come to earth, just as it is in Heaven. What greater hope can we have!

Activation Points:

1. What is the difference between the Biblical promised land and our own promised land today? Describe both.

2. What are the two main roles of man on earth?

3. Why has God given every person certain talents, gifts, and abilities. What are yours? List them.

4. What does going through difficult times have to do with your own promised land?

5. Give a description of what you think your own promised land might be.

CHAPTER SIX:

HELPFUL HINTS TO DISCOVERING YOUR PURPOSE

While we are spending a lot of time talking about fulfilling your purpose, it might be helpful to talk about some things you can do. Part of the message that is emphasized at History Makers Academy is how do we work within the area of our calling. Another part of the message is helping you find your purpose. It is not good to merely tell you to find your calling without giving you direction in how to find your calling. That is what we want to do now. I want to give you some hints that will clarify how you can better determine what God has gifted you to do.

1. Understand that your purpose is greater than you are.

Living for God and His purpose is always greater than living for yourself. It is better than living for your family. This is often where you will find the greatest strength to continue through the hard times. Many times, when I am at the end of my abilities, or at the end of my patience, it is only the idea that my purpose is so much bigger than I am that keeps me moving forward. It is the hope of His Kingdom coming that helps me find the reserves to keep fighting the good fight. It keeps me moving forward with the conviction that I can do all things through Christ who strengthens me.

It is important to remember that it is critical that you continue. You have to fight through to the end. When you understand your purpose it is easier to keep from getting distracted by the easy trails that crop up beside the road you are traveling down. That is where the saying, the grass is always greener on the other side of the fence, comes from. Everything looks easy when you are struggling with the path God has put before you. Everyone's pathway looks easier. You do not see their struggles; you only see their victories.

2. Have an undivided focus on Jesus.

Scripture says, "Fixing our eyes on Jesus, the Author and Perfecter of our faith." (Hebrews 12:2). The Greek word for fixing is *alfaro*, which means an undivided attention. Why do we do this? **When you fix your eyes on anything else but Jesus, you tend to be led to that thing and then your treasure becomes what that thing is.** But when you fix your eyes on Jesus, Jesus leads you in the right direction and causes you to be successful. When there is a fork in the road and you do not know where to turn, keep your eyes fixed on Jesus and He will lead you.

Think about when you were learning to drive. You were careful to put your hands in the right place. You adjusted the seat, put on your seatbelt, fixed the mirrors so you could see properly, and then you inserted the key into the ignition and started the car. As you drove, especially in those first days, you were very careful to look at the road ahead or in the mirrors.

Do you remember that every time you looked to the side of the road, or at the person sitting beside you that you tended to drive in the direction in which you were looking? That is why you are to fix your eyes on Jesus. It is easy to drift, even when you are doing everything right, except looking at the road in front of you. It is easy to miss the turn when your eyes are not fixed on Jesus. It is easy to get distracted by the radio, or the GPS, or anything else in the car. Keep your eyes fixed on Jesus.

3. Have a radical passion for your purpose.

This is why the devil uses depression in our generation to the extent that he does. Because if he can get you caring about nothing you will not be able to fulfill your purpose. **Passion is what separates superstars from the rest of us.** The professional athlete that is better than the rest is that way because of passion. At the height of his game Michael Jordan was considered the greatest basketball player alive. Everyone assumed it was all talent, a gift from God. Now, do not get me wrong, a lot of Michael's ability was a gift from God. During an interview about what it felt like to be the greatest basketball player alive and how it felt to be so gifted naturally Michael pointed out an important point that few people knew.

Michael told the reporter his secret. The essence is that when everyone else comes into the gym in time for practice Michael gets there an hour early and works out. When everyone goes home after practice, Michael stays an hour longer and continues to work out. What looks like natural talent is so much more!

What looks like natural talent is actually radical passion for being the best in the game. We need to have the same radical passion to be the best in whatever area we are called. We should approach our calling with the passion of Michael Jordan, gifted above all others by God, yet working harder than everyone around us to be the best in our field of expertise.

4. Be passionate about growing your gift.

They say that when Thomas Edison was trying to invent the light bulb he would go days without even eating and he would not notice. **If you can conquer your gifting, you can conquer the world because a gift makes room for a man the Bible says.** It also says, "You see a man that excels in his work, he will stand before kings." You rule in life through your gifting.

This is a lot like having radical passion. This passion to growing your gift comes in several forms. It means that you are constantly seeking to learn more about your area of calling or your gift. It means that you are a great student of what has happened in your area of gifting in the past.

Is your sphere of influence politics? Then you should study the men and women who have come before you in the position to which you feel called. Look at their speeches, their public appearances. Look at how they behaved in public meetings. Look at how they worded resolutions or laws. Study the problems they had getting a piece of legislation passed. Study how they built coalitions to get a law passed. Study their strengths and their weaknesses. Strengths will often get us to great places. What we fail to realize is that weaknesses can destroy us when we get to great places. Often a man's gift is enough to get him there, but if he has not conquered his weaknesses he will find it impossible to stay there. Never assume you are beyond weakness. If there is anything life teaches us, it is that every person has weaknesses. The strongest among us have weaknesses. We would all do well to tame our weaknesses so that they do not bring us down at the height of our success.

In other words, become the best student of your calling. Become the expert. Do not count on others to be the expert. You be the expert! You should be so passionate about your gift that no one is a greater expert than you on the areas concerning your gift.

5. Have a God-given desire to serve people; and serve them with your gift.

Some people are not successful because they are selfish. When you do not cultivate your tools and your gifts to serve the world, you are selfish. This is why Jesus called the steward who did not multiply his talents a wicked, unfaithful servant because he did not take what he had and grow it and multiply it. Your gift is the ultimate form of giving.

You must remember that there is nothing guaranteed, even in the area of your gifts. If you do not work, you will not eat from the fruit of your gift. If you do not sow, you will not reap. The mistake many of us make is that we think, because it is a gift from God, there are no requirements. How dare we sell God that short! How dare we think that there is some type of magic involved in fulfilling our calling. We are not talking about buying a lottery ticket. We are talking about serving the King of Kings and ruling and reigning in His Kingdom.

It has been said, "The harder I work, the luckier I get." Of course this is just a saying – we do not believe in luck. There is a lot of truth in this statement though in some ways. We think that gifted people achieve success without any work. Nothing could be further from the truth. The harder people work, the better they get at what they do. The harder you work the more you create opportunities for God to intervene on your behalf.

6. When you excel in your gifting, you portray the image of God.

Remember that Jesus said, "If you have seen Me, you have seen the Father." (John 14:9). The Bible also says that we have been made in the image and likeness of God (Genesis 1:27). How can you imitate God? You imitate God by fulfilling your purpose. God always fulfills His purpose and when you fulfill yours, you look like Him. When the world sees someone excelling in the thing that God gave them, they do not see you they see God. This is why you must be a good steward with what He has given to you.

You have heard it said that some times it is hard to hear the Gospel for the Christians. You are the only Jesus that many people will ever see. When you truly understand that, it will change how you interact with those around you. When you realize that you really are representing God, then you will work harder to do everything with excellence. Like a true servant of the King, you will make sure that you do nothing to embarrass the King. You will make sure that you do nothing to make the Kingdom look weak or foolish in the eyes of the world.

7. **It is impossible for you to love God and not love His people. If you get close to the heart of God, your heart is broken for people and you will use whatever tool you can, to reach them. If you don't love people, get into the presence of God. When you love on God, you begin to love on people.**

One of the best things about loving God and having a relationship with Him is that it makes you more like God. As you immerse yourself in His Word, His Word transforms you. As His Word transforms you, you find yourself better positioned to achieve greater influence in the sphere of influence in which God has called you. So, as you become more like God, you will find yourself loving people more. You will find yourself feeling compassion toward the lost and dying, instead of feeling judgmental. Being changed into the image of God in Christ Jesus means that you will see the lost world and hurt for it, rather than rejoice that people are lost and outside of the salvation that God so readily gives to you.

There is no greater measure of your success in this area than how you treat the people around you. Loving the least among you is a testimony to the changing power of the Gospel message. It is a testimony to those around you that God is working through you.

8. **Your gift is your key in loving people. Why do you go to church? You go to church so that God can train you, and so you can go out and love people.**

Faith, hope, and love abide, but the greatest is love (1 Corinthians 13:13). Everything in your life comes down to love. Love covers a multitude of sins. Love sets you free. Love reigns. **Perfect love casts out fear** (1 John 4:18). You see the power of love around you every day. You know the power of love. You know how it transforms hurting people into whole people capable of love and compassion. If you operate in your gift and do not love people, then you are not truly showing them God. If you perform miracles but do not have love, you are not operating in the realm that really transforms those around you and brings you into a place of full and complete influence in the area where God has called you.

Love opens the door and makes the way easier. People respond to love like they respond to nothing else in the Universe. When you walk in love and show it to those around you, you find them being drawn to you. Often they are drawn to you in spite of yourself.

Therefore, you understand that love transforms the Universe. It changes the hearts of kings. It changes the hearts of men. We all respond to love like no other force in the world. When you see love truly lived out, you know that a God of love exists.

Activation Points:

1. Give a few examples in life where God has shown you what your purpose is. Either through desires, gifts, dreams, or even prophecies.

2. For each of the "helpful hints" in chapter six, describe practically how you can make sure you are living by them. How will you fulfill them?

SECTION TWO:

UNDERSTANDING HIS KINGDOM

CHAPTER SEVEN:

JESUS – THE KINGDOM OF GOD IN FLESH

When we talk about the Kingdom of God, we are talking about His rule and His reign, that which is established in Heaven. There is perfection, life, joy, and everything that you could ever want. It is happening in Heaven because His Kingdom reigns freely there. The Kingdom of God in Heaven has full occupation of the Heavenly realm. The definition or way to describe the Kingdom of God is that it is comprised of two parts.

1. The King: Every kingdom needs a king. You cannot have a kingdom without a king. Therefore, the Kingdom of God has a king.

2. The King's domain. The Kingdom of God is the king's domain. How many people would want to be close to our King? How many would want to be in His domain? Well, you are not dead yet, but that is why John the Baptist was preaching and Jesus said that the Kingdom of God is near to you. That was a big deal. You rarely hear of Jesus preaching the Gospel of Salvation only, you hear of Him preaching the Gospel of the Kingdom, the rule of God.

Our job as citizens of a Kingdom that is in another realm is to make the earth become the King's domain because, at this point, it is not here yet to the extent that God desires. The heavens are the Lord's; the Earth has been given to us (Psalm 115:16). Our job as citizens of another empire is to bring the aspects of the Kingdom of God to the earth. So, the Kingdom of God is not here, but we are. We have been sent from an Embassy of Heaven and we are to bring the Kingdom, the King's domain, and set it up here on earth.

What do we call that in war? Conquering. It is important to remember that we are not talking about literal war. We are talking about spiritual war. We are talking about bringing love into your sphere of influence. We are talking about using your influence to break down the principalities and powers that reign over an area and bring them into submission to God and His Kingdom. We are talking about what Chuck Colson called "Kingdoms in conflict." We are bringing one kingdom into conflict with the existing kingdom in order to establish a new order to the kingdom.

For example, in the realm of entertainment we are talking about bringing, not just Christian music into the music industry, but we are also talking about quietly influencing the music industry with Godly principles and an incredible amount of skill. It is important to have both, the integrity and the skill, if we are going to truly influence the sphere of entertainment.

Nowhere on the face of this earth or anywhere in the universe is there an area, or region, that is absent of a kingdom. There is no kingdom-less place anywhere. Toronto is not kingdom-less, Philadelphia is not kingdom-less, there is a kingdom everywhere. It is either the kingdom of darkness or the Kingdom of Light. It is one or the other. So, our job is to literally bring His Kingdom upon the earth. You are literally going to spiritual war to dethrone the kingdom of Satan in order to enthrone the Kingdom of our Lord Jesus. For this reason, it is the Christian's duty and job to multiply, fill the earth, and subdue it. We are to go and multiply.

Luke 11:2-4

And He said to them, "When you pray say: 'Father, hallowed be Your name. Your kingdom come. Give us each day our daily

78

bread. And forgive us our sins. For we ourselves also forgive everyone who is indebted to us. And lead us not into temptation."

We know the Lord's Prayer also says, *"Your Kingdom come, Your will be done, on earth as it is in Heaven."* God's dream is for His Kingdom to be set up on the earth and for Jesus to be enthroned. What we are essentially doing is not talking about getting God to come and walk through the doors on a red carpet and everything is going to be okay. Before God's Kingdom can be established, another kingdom must be dethroned. Before God's Kingdom can be enthroned, another kingdom must be dethroned. That is a challenge.

I remember a few years ago I was part of a certain business endeavor. A number of Christians starting joining a particular company. The CEO was so impressed with these Christians' lives that he started incorporating Godly principles. He was not a Christian, he was not saved, he was not spiritual, but he started incorporating Godly principles into the company and the company began to have success. How could it be that he would begin benefitting from the Kingdom principles but not yet be a Christian? This is the power of the principles of this Kingdom. **The principles of the Kingdom of God are not limited to just believers.** The principles of the Kingdom belong to all who will take hold of them! Of course there is only one way to SALVATION and that is through Jesus Christ the King, yet all can benefit from the principles of that King.

When this particular CEO began adhering to the King's principles, he began to get some great results! Now all that was left was for this CEO to meet the King of these principles! When this man started to do things the Christian way the company began to have great success. The company began to experience blessing and the power of Satan began to become dethroned and some began to want to meet the King of the Kingdom! The process of dethroning Satan's domain had begun.

What does it mean to dethrone the kingdom of darkness and enthrone Jesus?

You are dethroning the reign of Satan and putting into place the Kingdom of God. This is the dominion of evil. When God uses you to heal the sick person, or you live by truth, you have dethroned the kingdom of darkness and ushered in another Kingdom through that healing or Godly lifestyle.

Everywhere in your sphere there is a kingdom that has been set up. This is the reason why Christians have not occupied the earth, because we have not brought that Kingdom yet to the degree that is necessary. We have the Kingdom of God in our churches very freely. If you go on a Sunday morning to church, you will see, feel, and experience the Kingdom of God. We have not often extended that same Kingdom beyond the four walls of the church.

What is the Kingdom of God in Jesus Christ?

John 1:16-18

For of His fullness we have all received of His fullness, and also grace upon grace. For the law was given through Moses, grace and truth were realized through Jesus Christ. No one has seen God at any time; the only begotten God who is in the bosom of the Father, He has explained Him.

Jesus Christ was (and is) the sum total of two things: Grace and Truth. Those two things make up the Kingdom of God in Jesus. This is very important. Grace being the Spirit, the manifestations of the Spirit – the healings, the prayer, the life, the spiritual. Truth being the values and the principles of the Kingdom.

The Kingdom of God in Christ Jesus was displayed in Spirit, (the Grace) via signs and wonders, power, miracles, ascension to Heaven, walking on water, and multiplying loaves and fishes etc. Now can that affect your work place in the world? Yes, to an extent it can. Generally, history has taught us, though, that signs and wonders alone are not enough to keep someone. Jesus operated in great grace, establishing the Kingdom through mighty signs and wonders and works of grace and of the Spirit. We are called to do this too! Grace is the empowerment, the divine power, and the miracles.

Grace and empowerment are great and Jesus went around walking in the Life of God this way, and told us that signs and wonders are to follow us! This is a work of grace in our lives. Jesus was full of grace, the manifestation of the Spirit. He was also full of Truth, which are the teachings, principles, and values of Jesus – the day to day lifestyle. Jesus walked in grace AND truth. The problem is, in the church today we tend to chase the spiritual or supernatural sometimes at the expense of the truth. We do not realize that living out truth can also be very supernatural and has the power to redeem society. So the Kingdom of God in Jesus is the sum total of the Spirit of Christ and the teachings of Christ through the Bible, the Spirit, *and* the Word of grace and truth.

This means that we must approach influencing society with a double-edged sword rather than just emphasizing one over the other. For example, there are times when the demonstration of the Spirit through prophecy or preaching is out of order in a political or professional setting. Sometimes choosing to love the truth and do right when others are choosing wrong is the best approach to establishing His Kingdom in a certain setting. This is actually why Jesus wanted us to be as shrewd as serpents. We must be wise and be strategic when it comes to influencing society. The manifestations of the Spirit of God have spiritual and supernatural power. The principles and teaching of Jesus also have spiritual and supernatural power.

Jesus carried both. The law was given through Moses. Jesus taught grace AND truth. In the New Testament we saw Jesus performing many extraordinary miracles and He was strong in Spirit but He also sat down and taught people how to live day to day. He taught love, giving, honesty, and even financial truths.

The Function of the Spirit of Christ

The Spirit of Christ brings restoration to man, the human being. So for example, you heard the Word of Faith and you mixed it with faith, you heard the Word of Salvation and you said I believe and literally something took place in you that you could not see. Miraculously, as a result of doing these things, your Spirit was regenerated, you were restored in spirit and now you are a Christian!

The Spirit of God restores the man and the principles of God restore the earth.

So, you are a Christian. The Spirit of God has transformed your inner man. You are working in a secular business. A business does not have a spirit or a soul. You cannot lead a business to salvation, but you can implement Christian principles into that business that restore the business to an image of Heaven or at least cause it to prosper.

It is life and lifestyle. Life is the life of God, but now you must walk out the lifestyle. So, you receive life and salvation, but now you have got to live by the principles and maintain the lifestyle to keep the life. The life of God restores you, the lifestyle of God changes the world. Some famous people are living the lifestyle without the life. Some famous people are doing both. For example, Bono is changing the world with his lifestyle. You have all these people living the lifestyle of the Christian, they are living the life.

In the church, we have been given the life, but some do not live the lifestyle of the Kingdom. One of the crucial reasons why we have failed in influencing the world with the Kingdom of God is because we have experienced the Spirit of Jesus but far too often we fail in living out the principles and lifestyle of Jesus.

When you break Kingdom laws and ignore the principles of the Kingdom of God in your country, the country begins to come under another kingdom. It begins to come under the kingdom of darkness. When you fail to honor the values and principles of the Kingdom of God in your home, eventually your home and family comes to ruin.

Matthew 28:20

...teaching them to observe all that I have commanded you, and lo, I am with you always, even to the end of the age.

Integrity! **Can you imagine a society where business is done with integrity? We would have Heaven on earth.** We would have honor! Can you imagine a society of honor? Picture a society of absolute honor; that is a teaching and principle of Jesus.

What about forgiveness! Picture a society established on forgiveness. I first observed these principles when I was going into unsaved people's homes and observing their marriages. I was learning why some unsaved people's marriages were better than some Christian marriages. If you look into any marriage that is failing, Christian or not Christian, it is not necessarily the absence of God, it is really the failure to adhere to the laws and principles that make for a happy marriage.

Now let's look at it on a national level. We were founded on Christian principles, that blessed us as a nation. What are some Kingdom laws we are breaking?

1. You shall not murder (Exodus 20:13) – yet we are murdering with abortion.

Surprisingly, the presence of churches in a city or nation does not necessarily mean the city or country is being changed. We can all think of nations or regions that have churches on every corner – yet we cannot say that the nation has been discipled according to the Great Commission. Jamaica is the ideal example of this principle. Jamaica has the most churches per capita of any nation, yet much of the society, is still suffering from systemic poverty, fatherlessness, and violence. We are not putting down any country here. We are merely trying to use a practical example of the principles we are talking about. Every country has its spiritual diseases. So the amount of Christians in one location or the amount of churches, neither necessarily affects how your country operates. You could have church services happening on Sunday morning all over the country, but if those same believers who attend church do not live out and establish the principles of the Kingdom in that society – the Kingdom will not come to that society.

There are many pastors and evangelists who operate in signs and wonders on a regular basis. Some of them even have thousands of members in their churches. Some of these same leaders who operate in grace and the gifts of the Spirit, however, actually do not adhere to the values of the Kingdom behind closed doors! Jesus came full of grace and truth, the reality of the foundation of the Word of God.

The church is supposed to be dictating how the society goes. We are to disciple nations!

The wages of sin is always death. Every time you sin, something in you dies, or something around you dies.

A nation is not great by the virtue of its wealth, rather a nation is great by the wealth of its virtues.

The founding father of Singapore understood this. He was not a Christian, but he would not let anyone work in the government who was cheating on their spouse. He understood that they were betraying a covenant. He understood that if someone is willing to betray the person closest to them, they will be willing to betray their government.

Principles establish a nation. A Scripture that proves this is, "Righteousness exalts a nation." (Proverbs 14:34). Righteousness and integrity are the foundation of his throne (Psalm 89:14). Not war, not necessarily a strong prayer life. Righteousness and integrity exalt and build.

You can eventually lose the life of God because you violate the lifestyle consistently and violate it with a hardened, unrepentant heart.

Jesus came full of grace, but also truth. **We need to establish truth in society no matter what sphere we are in.**

Consider a people group that really shows what we are talking about. The Jewish people. Although many of them reject Jesus as the Messiah (have not experienced salvation yet), their adherence to many Kingdom principles has prospered them. They are excelling in some of the top positions of influence. They are Noble Prize winners and the elites when it comes to wealth. This largely has to do with the Kingdom principles they practice, though they reject the King of that same Kingdom.

Nobody knew stewardship principles like Jesus did. He absolutely knew how to turn society upside down with the Spirit *and* the principles. The principles redeem the society and the Spirit redeems the soul.

It is time that Christian products and services become so much better than the world's offerings that people begin to seek us out. Instead, we find that many people lead with their faith as if they are hoping to manipulate us into accepting their substandard work because they are Christian. It should be the opposite. We should demand above standard work from Christians. We should settle for nothing less than the best from Christians. We should be telling those who provide substandard work that they are not presenting the Gospel in a manner we are willing to accept.

There is a story about Alexander the Great. He had conquered the known world and was growing restless. One night he was wandering around the edges of the camp and came upon a guard who was on the outer picket line, the edge of security. The guard was asleep. Alexander kicked the man and startled him awake. Realizing who was starring at him, the guard jumped to attention.

Alexander was extremely upset. "What is your name?" he demanded.

"Alexander, sir." The guard hoped desperately that sharing the name might be helpful.

Without pausing for even a moment, Alexander the Great looked at the guard. "Alexander, huh. Well, Alexander, let me give you some advice." The guard perked up, hoping that he would gain something of value from his namesake. **"Either change your conduct, or change your name!" Alexander the Great walked away.**

This is the advice that we need to give to many who claim the name of Jesus, the name of Christian. If you are not living in such a way that the Kingdom of God is advanced by your living, then change your conduct or change your name. If you are not living a life that is proudly showing the love of Jesus, then change your conduct or change your name. You cannot serve two masters.

Genuine societal transformation is based on the principles of the Kingdom of God and can be called organized righteousness. Societal transformation is not about just changing individual lives; it is about changing the way in which the culture responds to the principles of God. It is about changing drug addicts and alcoholics by the power of the Gospel, through programs that meet them on the street where they live. It is about teaching young men how to be fathers and how to take care of their families – even through the tough times.

Societal transformation is what we really need in order to fulfill the Great Commission. **We cannot think about discipling a whole nation with just great church services and evangelism alone!** The values of Heaven must become systemic in a nation to change the culture. It is no longer enough to merely lead people to Jesus in a religious service. Fewer and fewer people are willing to come to a religious service because of the abuses of religion around the world. People respond, however, to someone who is living out the Gospel message by working to transform society through their lifestyle rather than through their words.

Where the principles of the King are, the King will establish residence. It is only a matter of time until the King comes where His principles are established. This is why I believe Jesus as the King will not come and take up His throne on the earth, until the glory of the knowledge of God covers the earth. He will not come until the Kingdom of God covers the earth, and as the waters cover the seas. Am I saying the earth will have to be perfect, and a society of absolute Kingdom values established before the King will come? No. There should be an acceleration and an increase of the King's dominion on the earth and then the King comes and takes up residence. **He is not coming to take up residence in your church service only. He is coming to**

take up residence in the nations. He is coming to take up residence in media, He is coming to take up residence in government, and in every sphere of society, and Jesus wants to be King. His citizens must go in and take up residence and occupy. You must bring light where there is darkness. You must bring life where there is death. You must bring love where there is hatred. You must bring honesty where there is dishonesty. You must bring integrity where there is corruption. You must use your brain and systematize righteousness and bring organized righteousness to society in such a way that the place where you are is being blessed and the King can come.

There was a time when somehow we thought that just the two hours on a Sunday morning was going to transform the world. When it comes to societal transformation it takes more than that. Every believer must be willing to live out grace and truth beyond the four walls of the church to establish the Kingdom!

Activation Points:

1. What is the sum total of the Kingdom of God? Your answer should be two parts.

2. List five manifestations of the Spirit of God. Manifestations mean anything that is spirit or invisible. It may mean singing a worship song, or maybe healing the sick. It is spiritual; something that the Holy Spirit activates.

3. List five principles or values taught by Jesus Christ.

4. List at least five areas of society and a principle or value of Jesus Christ for each aspect of society (i.e. government, education, family), and connect a principle of Jesus like love, or the principle that it is more blessed to give than to receive; and connect a principle that would really benefit that area of society. For example, in

the business and the financial world, honesty and integrity would be in that category.

5. What is the difference between revival and societal transformation?

CHAPTER EIGHT:

THE LAWS OF THE KINGDOM OF GOD

Let's look at the balance of grace and truth. What does grace represent? **Grace represents the moving and manifestation of the Spirit.** That is why we pray, to access the spiritual realm and to move by the Spirit. What does truth represent? Truth represents the principles of God; the Word, the values that reform a society. It may sound simple but believe it or not, it is one of the most important concepts you will learn in your entire Christian life. It is also one of the least taught doctrines in the 21st Century Church. It is balancing the two that is so critical. Nations rise and fall based upon the church understanding that balance.

Matthew 28:18-20

*And Jesus came up and spoke to them, saying, "All authority has been given to Me in Heaven and on earth. **Go therefore and make disciples of all the nations**, baptizing them in the name of the Father and the Son and the Holy Spirit, **teaching them to observe all that I commanded you; and lo, I am with you always, even to the end of the age**." (Emphasis added.)*

It is also read as, "go and disciple nations, teaching them to observe." The goal and design of God is not just to see the Kingdom come in our own lives, but for the Kingdom to come in the nations, and into the whole earth, as we have discussed.

John 1:17

For the Law was given through Moses; but grace and truth were realized through Jesus Christ.

In the Old Testament, it was called the law, it was what you do or do not do. You did not want to break that law because you could be stoned to death, or reap some horrible disaster.

God used Israel very much as a prophetic type of what would be the New Testament church. When Israel went through the Red Sea it was a prophetic type of water baptism. Israel in the wilderness going to the Promised Land is a prophetic image of the Church in the wilderness and then headed to Heaven. In the same way, the sin issue, the wages of sin is death, was a great picture that sin equals death, unless you have the atonement of Jesus Christ. Even then nothing good comes out of sin. When you break the law, you break yourself. In the New Testament we do not call it the law necessarily, we call it the truth. For the rebel you need a law, for the slave you need laws, for the son you just give him truth and he follows it.

The son does not need laws. They that are led by the Spirit are the sons of God (Romans 8:14), and they are no longer under the law. You are not a slave to sin, you are a son. So, grace and truth were realized with Jesus Christ. If you are going to walk out the truth, you need the grace to do it. If you are going to function in grace, you need to know the truth.

This is the totality of the Kingdom of God as summed up in Jesus Christ. There are people who can call themselves Christians, and appear to be very spiritual, but are not actually living out the lifestyle. They have received the life. They have been saved, but they break Kingdom principles (Kingdom laws), and wonder why bad things happen to them. In the same way, when you function just in truth, lifestyle without the life, you do not have salvation. Or you function in just truth, but do not have the working of the Holy Spirit, helping you to do that, you cannot walk out truth to the best of your ability without the spirit. Grace and truth were realized through Jesus Christ.

Now let's look at the laws of the Kingdom. (Some might prefer to call them principles, to differentiate from the laws of the Old Covenant.) The Scripture says, righteousness exalts a nation (Proverbs 14:34). So there is a Kingdom law. What is the Kingdom law here? **Righteousness – when you practice the principle of righteousness it accomplishes something.** The Prime Minister of Japan said that Japan used to be a very underdeveloped country prior to the Second World War. The philosophy of the country at that time was, "Only fools do things right." Meaning, if you can cut corners and do it cheaply and get away with it, are you not the wiser person. To a human standpoint, it makes sense, does it not? If I can cheat you and get away with something, do I not come out the victor? That is why many cheap products were coming out of Japan and it was said if it was Japanese you did not want it because it would look good, but it would break two months later. What they discovered after going through a period of about 20 years when they became Americanized was a different way of doing business. This was the years after World War II. American influence started to change their thinking through education. Americans were going to Japan, teaching and establishing different mindsets and the Japanese philosophy began to change. America essentially brought over Christian values, or grace and truth. They brought over truth, principles, and values. The same values that they brought over to Japan are the same values that America was established on. America became the superpower that it is, or almost was, not because they were just that good, but because of the Christian values they were founded on. Not necessarily founded on grace or a great prayer meeting, but being founded on the principles of the Kingdom of God.

The principles are important, even if the life is not explicitly stated. Laws and principles govern every area of the Universe.

This is especially true concerning human lives and culture. We understand this. If you eat too much you will gain too much weight. If you smoke, you will develop health issues, everything from breathing problems to cancer. If you drink alcohol in excess, you will destroy your liver. These are examples of principles that we all understand. We know the consequences. We do not argue that this should not matter to us, we accept the consequences.

God's principles sustain a nation. They provide hope in a hopeless situation. This can be seen in our court systems. A country that has an independent judiciary branch is more stable than any country that has a judicial branch that does the bidding of the executive branch. There is no justice when principles and laws are not equally enforced. That was the entire point of the American Civil Rights Movement of the 50s, 60s, and beyond. Laws were being enforced. Unfortunately, if you were black or white mattered greatly in the outcome of a trial. African-Americans were given stiffer sentences for the same crime or often even for lesser crimes. There was not justice to be had and it affected every area of life in America. It took heroic actions by thousands of people to set the process on a better path. We are not saying that there are no longer racial issues in America, or elsewhere in the world, but it is clear that the world is better than it was because America started righting her course.

That is a classic example of the value of laws and principles that are based on Biblical standards even without the effects of a full blown revival.

Part of what Japan's philosophy became, "Do unto others what you wish others to do to you;" which is a totally different mindset than before. Over the next 20 years of applying principles like this one, they became the fastest growing economy in the world.

But now, look at America. On Wall Street, the corruption that is going on – look what it is doing to America. The lesson of America now is becoming a testimony that when you turn your back on Kingdom principles, when you walk away from honor, integrity, honesty, and the like, you will rapidly decline. This is not the way a culture should go.

Let's look at some Kingdom laws.

In this context when we use the term Kingdom "law" we are referring to Kingdom "principles. Just as there are laws that govern the material world, the natural realm, there are some *superior* laws that govern the spiritual world. There are laws in both the natural and spiritual realm. In the natural realm there is the law of gravity, and in the spiritual realm there is the law of sowing and reaping, and the law of righteousness, for example. As humans, we were designed to function within both realms and adhere to both sets of laws.

Because we have an earthly suit, a material body, we have to observe material laws, unless we function in a spiritual law and override the natural realm law. Jesus did this. One minute He is eating fish and He does not want to get too close to the fire because He might get burned, and the next minute He is walking on water. He had to observe both laws the same way we do. We have to take care of our bodies, we have to go to sleep at a decent hour and we have to eat right. In the same way, we have to be able to access divine power and great grace, through the Spirit of God through prayer exercises.

We tend to lean more toward observing earthly laws and we break spiritual ones. This explains why the Bible says the wages of sin is death. I used to think that God did not want me to sin because it made Him angry. I thought it was because, somehow, He was egotistical. I thought He needed us to obey Him because He is the great God. Are you ready to hear this? In actuality God does not want you to break laws because He loves you. He designed you as a citizen of a kingdom to function at your best within the parameters of Kingdom laws. He knows how you were made and designed to function. So, when God instituted the law of honoring the Sabbath day, that is not just because He wants you to take a day off, it is because He knows how your body was meant to function. When He says you need to laugh a lot it is because it is medicine to your bones (Proverbs 17:22). Science has discovered that when you laugh a lot, your immune system goes up. You are better able to fight off bacteria and sickness and you are physically well.

God knows how you were made to function. You were made to function according to Kingdom law. Imagine if Christians made learning Kingdom laws their highest priority and then instituted them in every sphere of society. So, when I approach the guy who drinks a lot and is a semi-alcoholic, I do not say to him, "You need to quit drinking or you're going to go to hell." He is already in hell as far as he is concerned. I am going to tell him about joy, I am going to tell him Kingdom principles. I am going to give him Truth and let him experience the Grace to walk it out later when he receives Jesus.

So the wages of sin is death, does not mean God is saying, "I'm angry because you've sinned, and now I'm going to kill you." God is actually saying, "No! If you sin, you're working against your own being, and breaking Kingdom laws (principles) will in turn break you." For example, you might say, "I don't believe in gravity," just like they say, "I don't believe in God and Your Kingdom laws," If you say that you do not believe in gravity and then you walk off a ten-story building, you are going to find out that, in spite of your lack of belief the law of gravity exists, it will break you. In the same way, the unsaved are doing this every day. They say, I do not believe in truth, I do not believe in righteousness, I do not believe in salvation, I do not believe in pro-life. They are breaking themselves in the end. To sin is really to violate Kingdom laws. Sin is a violation of Kingdom laws, just like trying to defy gravity, you are trying to violate a

Kingdom law. Violating any law, spiritual or material, is going to break you. There is no avoiding the consequences of the law.

The principle is this: *Wherever Kingdom laws are absent or are being broken, something begins to die.* You can see this in governments at the national level. The state of a country is a reflection of the Kingdom laws they are keeping or violating at the highest level. Right down to the pathological liar. Show me a liar, I will show you someone who is physically not well, who does not have many good relationships, who suffers from a number of other disorders, and is unhappy. Furthermore, if they are in a place of influence, they will not be there after a while. Show me somebody who breaks laws of integrity and does not do business with integrity. People end up wanting to avoid him like the plague. The very thing you are trying to cheat and break to gain wealth, wealth is now running from you because you did not love integrity. God made this clear in wisdom. If you love wisdom, then wealth, favour, and long life are yours. **Wisdom cries out, "Wake up and learn the truth; the truth will make you free."**

Have you ever been to Hastings Street in Vancouver? It is a long street of drug addicts and prostitutes. Literally, you can be on one street in Vancouver and it looks normal. You turn a corner onto Hastings Street and you think you have entered another world. This is about as good a picture of the absence of Kingdom law as you can find on the earth.

Any kind of social disorder in the extreme, whether it be disease, corruption, fornication, or what have you, is the absence of Kingdom law. In your family, if there is depravity or destruction in any way, there is a law that is being violated; laws of love, or laws of selfishness, etc.

Look throughout the city and identify some Kingdom laws that are being broken in your region or nation. Abortion – the law and value of life is being defiled, so you are breaking the country. You do not need any other argument; you are breaking the country.

Picture a global society of absolute abortion. This would be the end of all life!

As much as many are suddenly reticent to admit it, same-sex marriage is a violation of the truth. It is a violation of Kingdom law. The effects of this brokenness can be easily seen in the lives of those who practice this iniquity. Picture a society of absolute homosexuality. In a matter of a generation there would be no one left alive. Homosexuals cannot reproduce, therefore this generation becomes the last. The fact that we are developing science that makes a man and a woman unnecessary to the process does not mean that the principle of one man and one woman is not valid. It just means that we have managed to build one more Tower of Babel that God has yet to destroy.

Adultery and faithfulness. Picture a society of absolute adultery. The first casualty of such a culture is trust. The core of a family is the trust that is developed through the intimate relationship of a husband and a wife. This develops into a safe space for the children to be raised and to grow. A culture that permits only open sexual relationships will never have a stable family unit. It is impossible! The nature God created into male and female is such that monogamy is man's highest functioning state. That does not mean we are not tempted to be unfaithful. It means it is against the nature of who God created us to be. It is against the law God has placed in our heart.

The fact that most animals do not practice monogamy is not a compelling argument. First, animals do not live in the same sphere as humans. They do not have a spirit. God created man and woman to rule over the earth, animals included.

In an adulterous society, someone can come in your house and have sex with your sister. Imagine a city where there is absolute adultery, where adultery and fornication rule. What other devastations would emerge? Disease. Single parent pregnancy. Abortion. Look at all that is coming out of the heterosexual violation of the sanctity of marriage. Murder. Jealousy. The family unit would be broken. Divorce would be rampant. Just from that one Kingdom violation!

Now, try to imagine a world where there is absolutely no presence of God, a world where there are no Godly principles to guide anyone. That is hell! It is not something we should take lightly. **We should tremble to our core at the thought of a world so devoid of Heaven's breath.**

Do you see the issues created by kingdom laws being violated? Are you seeing yourself as having the answers to the building of all of life? You are that answer because you have the Bible, the book filled with the principles that can rebuild a society!

Picture a society of absolute dishonor of father and mother. Well, that is actually what we currently have. That is how Woodstock came about, rebellion against authorities. It was a literal movement of rebellion. What results came from that? Pregnancy, disease, drug abuse, suicide, death, broken homes, witchcraft, just everything came out of that movement. It affected multiple generations. In fact, we are still seeing the affects of the Woodstock generation. Free love, no boundaries, experimenting with drugs, living together without the commitment of marriage, all of these stated goals of the Woodstock generation are still destroying lives in the western world.

That generation ultimately went to college and got degrees. Many of them, instead of going into the corporate world and chasing money, went into education. They are now professors at many of our universities. They are teaching our children. They did not change their thought processes. They did not have a conversion experience. They are teaching about detachment from the morals that held our parents in check. They are teaching that outdated boundaries, like heterosexual marriage, should be destroyed. Do not be deceived, this is not some isolated incident – it is cultural revolution that has become cultural change!

Think about a world of lying instead of integrity. A society with zero integrity would self-destruct. Any business, or any person, who lacks integrity will be destined to decline from success to nothing. They are doing well one day and then gone the next! It is just a matter of time. What you are working to cover up when you are breaking these laws is going to expose you.

Look at a world where pornography is treated as if it were normal. Pornography is what the Bible says is going down to the pit, the pit you cannot return from. You are breaking laws and you will be sabotaged for that. We are witnessing the breaking up of families due to the evils of pornography. We are witnessing pedophilia like never before. One of the reasons for this is that we have come to think of the human body as a commodity, rather than thinking it is a gift from God to be treasured, guarded, and kept from evil. The end result is a world where we are actually debating whether it is normal for adults to have sex with young children.

Let's look at the health sector. A famous surgeon said that he discovered God through the medical field. He said that 75% of all physical sicknesses are related to the invisible moral laws of the Bible. His conclusion was that if people obey the moral laws, they can actually experience better health.

We must take this Gospel message to the world. Not just the message of salvation, though some of us are called to do just that, but also the message that God has business principles that will lead to success. God has principles of health that will revolutionize your mental and physical health. God has sexual values that will exalt your family. God has entertainment ideas that will change the way we view television or the movies or books. We must take the Gospel to the streets and to the board rooms of the entire world!

It is true that the whole Bible is literally a blueprint for how you were made to function. Even the old laws, that the Jews still abide by, bring them success. Even the laws on what to eat and what not to eat, those laws still work. That is why Jesus said, "I did not come to abolish the law, I came to fulfill it."

In Heaven, Kingdom laws are always abided by and never violated. That is part of what He was talking about when Jesus said, "Let Your Kingdom come, let Your will be done on earth, as it is in Heaven." (Mathew 6:10). You have the secret to prosperous businesses. You have the secret to your workplace becoming better. You have the secret to a healthy family life. Kingdom laws reinstate the earth back to what it was originally to be, a prototype of Heaven.

Let's take a look at Toronto, Canada. Toronto has exchanged Christian principles and a Christian God, for foreign gods. Let's say someone comes from another country, and they serve certain idols and gods in that country. They left their home country because of the property, the disease, and they came here to have a better life. They came here to have a better life because of the principles and values that caused Canada to be great and provide a better life for them. Then once here, try to enforce the observation of their religious practice at the expense of the values of Christianity. The very values that caused our nation to be blessed are suddenly "offensive" to those wanting to institute the practice of idol worship. The same worship of idols kept them in poverty and disease in their previous homeland for so many years!

This is not bigotry or racism. This has nothing to do with skin color, it has everything to do with, "Choose today whom you will serve. I put before you a blessing or a curse." (Deuteronomy 11:26). Pick the God of the blessing and the values He stands

101

for, and you get blessed. Choose the gods of Babylon and you get cursed. The movement of tolerance has become so huge that we do not know how to stand up for what we believe in!

Bestiality and necromancy, these are practices that are being introduced, that you can choose whether you are man or a woman, and choose what washroom you want to go into. They are teaching it in the school system today. You can see where this is going for society. Where is the moral line drawn? In the name of tolerance and freedom of choice, we are hurling toward anarchy at an unprecedented rate, unless spiritual salt and light enters into the equation.

These statements sound extreme, but they are not. We know they are true because we know that when the laws of the Kingdom of God are ignored, there is a deterioration that is unmatched in its depravity. The absence of the presence of God is a terrible reality. We can barely comprehend it. Yet, we are headed toward it with a passion that is unmatched in the history of the world. No civilization has faced such a rapid race toward a godless reality. Ancient Rome, for all its depravity, did not shake its fist in God's face the way we are. They were a nation based in pagan beliefs, so it is no surprise that they chose the belief in pagan gods over Jesus. We are nations professing to believe in Jesus and are suddenly embracing paganism like never before. How can we imagine that we will not be cast into a hell on earth by driving out the presence and stability of God?

Look at the education system. These shootings in our schools are an absolute phenomenon. It should be studied. They removed the Ten Commandments, the law, which is the truth. They removed prayer from schools, which is grace. And what do we teach? As soon as there is an absence or removal of the Kingdom of God, another kingdom rushes in.

In the *absence* of righteousness, a nation plummets. **Any society will eventually fall apart, if they choose to not abide by Kingdom principles.**

Even primitive societies seek to discover these moral laws and live by them. You can find remote tribes who are bowing down and worshipping idols made of wood and stone. They have never been touched by a theologian or missionaries, and they are worshipping the unknown God. Kingdom law is written within their hearts. In fact, there is one common thread you will find in almost every one of those kinds of tribes, and it is a particular law; blood sacrifice, the exchange of life for life. This is a Biblical principle found in the Old Testament; Life for life. It is written in their hearts.

Ecclesiastes 3:11

He has made everything appropriate in its time. He has also set eternity in their heart[s], yet so that man will not find out the work which God has done from the beginning even to the end.

Ecclesiastes says He has put eternity in their hearts so that they might know Him. Meaning, it is written in your DNA that there is a God. These things are written within our DNA, just like a computer. A society of absolute sexual immorality will self-destruct, or a society of absolute hate will self-destruct. The same is true of any culture built on the absence of the principles of the Kingdom.

The principles the church is carrying are the only things keeping the world together. This is why just bringing people to church is not enough. Jesus said in Matthew 28, when He gave the greatest commission, the greatest instruction that He *ever* gave; He said, "Go and disciple people, nations, systems, organizations, governments, workplaces, schools, families, teaching them to what… observe – teaching them to observe." It is not even that they get saved, but just teaching them to live by a different set of values. We are to instructed to preach the Gospel, but we are commanded to teach the nations to observe. Living and observing then leads to repentance and salvation.

You can have all the prayer meetings you want, but if you do not live out these values and enforce them, you will never truly bring the Kingdom of Heaven to earth.

It is time to redeem the land. It is time to bring the earth back to God.

Activation Points:

1. What are Kingdom laws (Kingdom principles) and why is it necessary to fulfill them?

2. What do the Scriptures mean when it says, "Righteousness exalts a nation?" (Proverbs 14:34).

3. Is it possible for a non Believer to get the blessing that comes with adhering to Kingdom laws?

4. Make a list of some Kingdom laws that you might be breaking in your life. What kind of results are you getting because of this?

5. Explain the statement, "Prayer alone is not enough to transform a society."

CHAPTER NINE:

JESUS, AND THE LIFESTYLE OF THE KINGDOM OF GOD

Luke 17:20-21

Now having been questioned by the Pharisees as to when the kingdom of God was coming, He answered them and said, "The kingdom of God is not coming with signs to be observed; nor will they say, 'Look, here it is!' or, 'There it is!' For behold, the kingdom of God is in your midst."

Here is the fascinating thing about this, that Jesus was not talking to believers. He was speaking to the Pharisees. Those who were not saved, but He is still saying the Kingdom of God is within you!

When you read Ecclesiastes for example, He says, "He has put eternity in their heart." (Ecclesiastes 3:11). Meaning, they have it written in their wiring that there is a God, an eternal God. What am I saying? The nature of the Kingdom of God has been hard wired into your being!

It is ego that stops people from coming into the Kingdom of God. It is easier for a camel to go through the eye of the needle than it is for a rich man to enter the Kingdom.

It is literally written in their hearts. An atheist, when his/her spouse is stricken with cancer, will say a prayer, just in case. "Eternity is written in their hearts."

There is no way to live independently of the Kingdom of God and be happy! Even if you are a Christian, if you neglect certain laws of the Kingdom, you are really only fooling yourself, and hurting yourself.

You cannot deceive the Kingdom of God. You can even get away with violating some principles in this life, but you blink your eyes and you are in the next life – the Kingdom of God's court system is able to judge.

For example, there was a particular man who stole a lot of money from a bank. The authorities were chasing him all over the world. They caught him and put him in prison. Once while being interviewed for mass media he said to them, "Thank God I am caught."

And they asked him, "How can you say that? You were rich and now you are in prison."

He answered, "I have more peace now that I am in prison than I did when I was on the run outside, always looking over my shoulder."

The absence of the Kingdom of God and the breaking of Kingdom laws produces a lack of peace and a lack of life. It takes your life. Both science and nature agree that when we obey the laws of God, Biblical and moral, we live a good life. It is a good way to live.

Both science and nature agree that when we obey the laws (principles) of God, we live a good life. We have these laws, they are written, they are carried in our Bible. Science is actually discovering God. The truly wise man is one who can merge science and Biblical truth to reveal God. We are to merge our sphere of rulership to bring a revelation of God in a community.

Our goal is to reveal Jesus, the King and His Kingdom, in everything we do. The Bible says the Kingdom of God is righteousness, peace, and joy in the Holy Ghost. When you break God's principles and laws, you lose these three things. When you break Kingdom law, you lose your joy, you lose your peace, and you lose your right standing with God. This is why the heathen lifestyle never truly satisfies. Those who do not live Kingdom lifestyle often turn to alcohol, drugs, and pleasure to replace the satisfaction you can only get by abiding by Kingdom principles. The sinful lifestyle is really an attempt to fill the void the world has inside of themselves, because they do not know Jesus or His values. The life of partying and addiction is a great deception, because a person wakes up the next day searching to find righteousness, peace, and joy. They have broken the laws that lead to natural righteousness, peace, and joy, so they settle for a false reality.

They do not realize that when Jesus says to the woman at the well, "I can give you a drink and you will never thirst again." (John 4:13). He is not talking about a high, He is talking about a lifestyle. He is talking about a consistency of living He is saying I can give you water and bread to eat where you will hunger no more. I can solve the cravings within you that are driving you to destroy yourself for the sake of a peace that you cannot find. You will become a human being like you have never experienced before, the Kingdom of God is within you!

They are looking for God and you have the road map. This is a different way of witnessing the Gospel message.

The Lordship of Jesus is not in order to be a dictator over us, but to prevent us from self-destruction. He knows how we were designed to function, because He designed us!

God said in His word, "I put before you today blessing and a curse, choose one." (Deuteronomy 11:26). I take no pleasure in anyone who dies. Why would you choose death? I put before you blessing and a curse. You can keep on cheating and deceiving yourself. You are breaking Kingdom laws and destroying yourself. **We must see sin as a violation against our nature.** Every time you sin, something in you or around you dies. Sin continually pays wages. All these abortions in our country are polluting the land. There is blood in the land that needs to be atoned for. It needs to be repented of.

Let this encourage each of us. If the Kingdom is within us, then we only need to find a way to live according to what God has placed inside each of us. That is why it is important to find your gifts and calling. That is why it is important to understand who God made you to be. What did He make you to do? How can you fulfill your mission in life?

We are all given a mission. It is within us, part of the Kingdom of God that is within us. When we work with God to fulfill our mission, we are actually releasing the Kingdom of God that is within us. We are actually bringing the Kingdom of Heaven to the earth in fulfillment of the Lord's Prayer.

There is no greater place for us than in the middle of what God created for each of us. We should not be envious of others' gifts or callings. We should never look at someone else's calling and covet it. God made us specifically for what He called us to. We have to understand that other callings come with other pressures. They come with other struggles. It does not matter how green the grass looks in someone else's field, God has called each of us to our field(s). Plow the ground that is before you. Work the field God has given you. The place of peace and fulfillment is in your own piece of ground that God prepared just for you.

Let's take a look at some Kingdom lifestyle principles:

Unforgiveness. You have probably heard it said that unforgiveness is like drinking poison and expecting the other person to die. In actuality, secular studies have proven that unforgiveness literally destroys your body over time.

Unforgiveness can be the cause of arthritis, intestinal problems, bowel problems, heart problems, allergies, and more.

Gratitude is the feeling of being thankful, appreciative, and grateful. Gratefulness is a significant Kingdom lifestyle principle. Life is going to have good and bad. There are two types of people, those who see the glass half empty and those who see the glass half full. The danger of seeing the glass half empty, even if it is a reality, is that you can poison your body by meditating on that. This is especially true of complaining. Complaining actually releases something in the atmosphere so much so that those who grumbled in the wilderness, God killed them all (Numbers 14:29). He did this because grumbling spoils the pot. God hates grumbling!

Recently, gratitude became a major study in mainstream psychology, because of its profound effects on the human being. Science has proven that people who are more grateful have higher levels of well-being. Euphoria can bring something good. Things are bad, but I feel good. My car broke down but I have a house. You know, my wife is mad at me, but she looks beautiful, or at least I have a wife.

Science has now proven that grateful people are happier, less depressed, less stressed, and have more of a sense of satisfaction with their lives.

Laughter comes from God. Joy comes from God. Peace comes from Him. It is of His nature. It is the way He is. It is His character. God is the God of faith. Satan is the author of fear. Satan invented fear. Because Satan is fearful and he wants you to be fearful too. Fear does not come from God. Anxiety is never from God. Anything that is contrary to the fruit of the Spirit should be approached with aggression in your life, until the principles of the Kingdom rule within your life.

Gratitude is a force!

One experiment found that customers of a jewelry story who were called and thanked for their purchase showed a subsequent 70% increase in purchases. Customers who were not called at all did not show any increase. The studies showed the value of acts of gratitude.

A famous Jewish psychiatrist, who is unsaved, said that 75% of patients would not have ended up in a psychiatric hospital if they understood the principle that he discovered in the New Testament, not the Torah. It astonished him. He quoted it like this, "It is more blessed to give than to receive." It actually has a profound effect on mental health.

I have suffered with bouts of anxiety in my life and I find that when I go out and give, it overcomes the anxiety. I actually use it as a relief. It is behavior modification.

You cannot deceive the Kingdom of God within your body.

Unforgiveness and negative thoughts are troubling. So, if there are secret sins in your life that no one sees, your body knows it. That is where guilt comes from. When you feel a sense of heavy guilt, you feel bad. King David described it as a groaning. He groaned because of his sin. He lay on his bed and he groaned (Psalm 6:6). He could tangibly feel the effects of sin within his body. He could actually feel it, the guilt. Whether you are saved or not saved, this truth applies to you. Jesus said to the Pharisees, "The Kingdom of God is within you!" (Luke 17:21).

The dominating kingdom that you cultivate within you will be what drives what you become. Some people live their entire lives angry at someone else. What a tragic way to live!

The Bible says that we are to renew our minds through the water of the washing of the Word (Ephesians 5:26). The Word literally, the Bible, His law, is a regenerating and restoring substance. The Bible actually has the power to reset your mind. You can and should be renewing your mind with it daily.

You should be in the Word every day. It's like medicine. Like an athlete working every day to improve his/her skills, you can be regenerating your mind and strengthening your spirit.

True education and study is man discovering the laws of God. This is true even in the realm of money. Do you see a millionaire who has made his money honestly? He is following laws that God invented. As he walks out his life by them, he is functioning in wisdom.

We train and equip with Kingdom principles. We show people how the things that are being studied are already in the Bible. The everyday practice of this helps to introduce people to the nature of the God they have not met. In this way, people are being introduced to the traits of the Kingdom.

When you truly discover the values of the Kingdom, you will read your Bible through a different lens.

Activation Points:

1. Choose thirteen values. For each value, list a physical effect that adherence to that value produces, and list an effect that the breaking of the value causes.
    For example: Gratitude. If I show gratitude, my body will do [this]. The opposite is complaining, so if I complain all the time, my body will do [this].

CHAPTER TEN:

THE NECESSITY OF FRUITFULNESS IN THE KINGDOM OF GOD

This is the time of the harvest, where God is looking to send forth sons and daughters who are not selfish, but they are selfless. God is looking for selfless sons and daughters who will bring forth the fruit of the Kingdom of God.

This harvest has been a long time coming. For generations the church has increased itself with only passing influence on the culture around it. It is now time for us to go beyond the four walls. It is time that we bring the power of integrity back into the market place. It is time we bring the power of love back into the government arena. It is time we bring the power of truth back into the media. It is time we do more than enrich ourselves through our work.

We need a generation of Christians who are sold out to the Kingdom. We need a generation who are willing to truly lay down their lives for the King. Men and women, sons and daughters who will serve the Kingdom in whatever area their calling is. Sons and daughters who will go out into the world and exert the influence of the Kingdom over the sphere of influence where they are called.

When that happens we will see a harvest like we have never seen before. We will see a harvest of nations rather than a harvest of communities. During the Great Awakening whole communities were changed by the power of the Kingdom of God. Now is the time for whole nations to be changed by the power of the Kingdom of God. Now is the time for us to step into our inheritance as sons and daughters and bring the King of Kings back into government, education, the arts, the media, entertainment, business, the church, and the family.

Just imagine the revolution that would create, having a nation being discipled by someone who is sold out to the principles of the Kingdom of God. Imagine the influence we could have, if only we would die to our own wants and dreams and live in His Kingdom completely.

We are going after results now, bringing forth the fruit of the Kingdom of God.

Matthew 21:43

Therefore I say to you, the kingdom of God will be taken away from you and given to a people, producing the fruit of it.

These are hard sayings about the Kingdom of God. The Kingdom can be given and the Kingdom can be taken. I want to be clear that I am not talking about salvation, but about the Kingdom. One look around our societies, and one can easily see that the Kingdom has been taken away. You, who have the Kingdom, never let it be taken from you. When something has been given to you, but then it has been taken back, it might be because you took it for granted. This Scripture reveals that to have received, automatically means that you have a responsibility to produce fruit. God says the Kingdom will be taken from you and given to another nation producing the fruit thereof, if you do not value that Kingdom.

Therefore, we understand that once we have the Kingdom of God, (we are not saying salvation), but those who have the Kingdom of God, have a requirement and responsibility to produce fruit. You have a requirement to produce some kind of result. There is no way you can truly say I am a part of the Kingdom of God and not bear fruit.

Every living thing on the face of the earth produces fruit after its own kind. That is one of the scientific laws that God established at the foundation of the Universe. Monkeys produce monkeys. They do not produce fish. Everything produces after its own kind. The same is true of the spiritual realm as well. True believers create true believers.

As we work in the area of our gifts and calling, we will produce fruit after our own kind. That means that if I am working in the government, creating just laws and just enforcement of laws, I will produce others who do the same thing. My one body working justice in the government will grow into many bodies producing justice. That is when we will see change in how government functions. That is when we will see positive change in the government.

We cannot produce fruit if we do not plant ourselves where we are called. If I am called to the area of entertainment, but spend my life in education, I will never produce the level of results I could if I worked in my area of calling. Again, this is why it is so important for us to discern what God has gifted and called us to do. That is why it is such a sad state to learn that very few people ever step up to learn where they are gifted and what they are called to do.

Let's look at difficult sayings of the Kingdom:

1. It is better to have not had the Kingdom of God than to have it and lose it.

It is unacceptable to have received the Kingdom of God and not do anything with it.

We, who have received, have an obligation to do something with the Kingdom of God. Think of the torment a person would go through who entered the Kingdom, tasted the fruit thereof, and then had it taken away. Think what it would be like for someone, who experienced the peace that passes understanding, to lose it.

Often we do not know what we have until it is gone. That is the Kingdom of God for some. We get used to the peace and the joy and if we were to lose that, we would find ourselves in a place of fear, pain, and depression.

Let us make sure that we obtain the Kingdom of God, and that we bear the fruit thereof, so that we do not have to experience the agony of losing the Kingdom.

2. The requirement of your citizenship in the Kingdom of God is to bring forth fruit from it.

You need to bear the fruit thereof. You say, "I am a citizen of the Kingdom of God." If you are saved, you must bear the fruit of salvation, which is the fruit of being a productive member of the Kingdom of God. Citizenship must be proven by living it out. We have talked about how, if your lifestyle does not prove that, then you are not bringing forth fruit of the Kingdom of God. Some people have a doctrine of "once saved always saved." And some people in this doctrine erroneously believe, "Now that I am saved, it does not matter what my fruit is." I am sorry, but God is just too smart for that! You can be saved and still have the Kingdom of God taken from you. Let everyone be clear on the distinction between salvation and His Kingdom.

Look at the parable of the talents. What happened when the person did not bear fruit? The talents were taken away (Mathew 25:14-30). So, therefore, the requirement of your citizenship in the Kingdom of God is to bear fruit.

The good news is that when God gives you talents, He also gives you the gifts and calling to learn how to use those talents to further His Kingdom. He is not a task master. He is a shepherd leading His flock. God gives gifts and He gives talents, and He gives opportunities to use them. Our one responsibility is to do everything in our power to develop the talents, the gifts, and the calling God has given us. The principles of the Kingdom mean that as we apply ourselves to learning how to do what we are called to do, we will be able to learn how to be the best we can in our area of calling.

3. The demand of the Kingdom of God is either 100% or no commitment at all.

Jesus said it, "No one, after putting his hand to the plow and looking back, is fit for the kingdom of God." (Luke 9:62). Think of the pearl of great price. The man sold all he had just to buy the one pearl (Mathew 13:45-46). The same is true with the treasure in the field, the man sold all he had just to buy the field (Mathew 13:44). Just to have the Kingdom of God, you simply need to seek first the Kingdom of God and all the rest finds its way to you (Mathew 6:33). The demand of the Kingdom of God is for either 100% commitment, or no commitment at all.

As you begin to excel in the area of your calling, the fruit of the Spirit will then begin to spread. The spread of kindness is a good thing. The spread of love will change entire areas of influence. The spread of joy will change the lives of everyone who comes into contact with joy. Peace will make the world a better place for everyone. Where there is peace there will be a better life for everyone in the area.

It is not magic. It is simply the earth and human relationships working the way that God created them to work. It is everything working according to the owner's manual. When everything in an area works properly, it works with less effort, it produces greater fruit, and it helps other areas work more efficiently.

4. He brought you to the Kingdom because He needs you to help Him.

John 15:16-17

You did not choose Me, but I chose you, and appointed you that you would go and bear fruit, and that your fruit would remain, so that whatever you ask of the Father in My name He may give to you. This I command you, that you love one another.

He brought you into the Kingdom of God not just for you, but because He needs you to help Him. So, a good Scripture demonstrating this is "Loose the donkey, the Master has need of him." You have been set free to be used of God. Think about that. You think you chose God and you are doing Him a favor. Rather He says, "I chose you and appointed you to do something about it, and to do something with it." He wants you to bring forth fruit that remains – real fruit.

Think about fruit for a moment. Fruit has the ability to enhance and sustain life. It contains essential vitamins for the body. Without fruit, humans have vitamin deficiencies that cause us to be less healthy. Fruit is a natural by-product of a tree or a vine doing what it was designed to do. The apple tree does not have to work hard to produce apples. It does not have to pray that apples will grow. It does not do anything, except exist in good health. A healthy apple tree will produce apples.

That is how we should be. A healthy son or daughter will produce fruit in keeping with the gifts and calling of our life. We will produce fruit that changes the sphere of influence where we are planted. We will produce fruit that makes the world a better place, fruit that helps people live happier, healthier lives. All of this happens when we are faithful to be who God created us to be.

5. You do not decide on what condition you live in the Kingdom.

You were created for His service, not He for yours.

We are better than that. Or at least we should be. The Bible says that those whom the Lord loves, He disciplines (Hebrews 12:6-11). That means that we should be ready to hear the hard Word. We should be ready to fight for what we believe in. What a shame it is that radical Muslims are more willing to live and die for their faith than some of us are.

We will see our influence grow when we get to the place that God can discipline us and we continue to move forward with the statement of saints before us: "Yet though He slay me, I will follow Him." (Job 13:15). We should get to the place where the hymn, *I Have Decided To Follow Jesus*, is our battle cry: "No turning back, no turning back."

When we get to that place, then, and only then, will we see the world changed by our presence. Then, and only then, will we see our influence grow beyond our wildest dreams in ways we cannot even imagine. There is no greater testimony to the power of God, than flawed people living a flawless life of service and sacrifice

6. Church attendance alone is not commitment to the Kingdom of God.

Some people treat their commitment to God like church attendance. It is like a library card that you received when you were young. You paid for it and you are registered at the library. You have your card – you have gotten your photo on it. Then for a decade, you never went back to the library. But you have your card, and you say to yourself, "I am reserved at the library." But you do not go and read. Unfortunately, too many do that with salvation. We think that because we got saved a long time ago, that we can just go on living in any way we please with no responsibility.

Jesus is not just a Savior to beggars. Jesus is a King who empowers. He does not just save you. He leads you. He empowers you. He enthrones you. He makes you someone who bears fruit for the Kingdom of God. So, you say, "I can't fast. I don't have time to pray. I'm too busy." If you are too busy to fast and pray, and you think you are fruitful, you are really just busy and thinking vainly.

Let's look at vanity. Vanity is the opposite of the spirit God has for us. He wants sons and daughters who are consumed with love for Him and His Kingdom. He wants sons and daughters who are so unimpressed with themselves, almost to the point as if they were not alive. I am reminded of the Apostle Paul, "To live is Christ, to die is gain." (Philippians 1:21). If we can understand that one Scripture, we can become who He called us and gifted us to become. If we can truly learn that vanity will destroy us and separate us from Him, then we can begin to change the world.

7.   He saved us so that we could go, not sit and relax.

This is because fruit bearing is not an overnight phenomenon. Think about that. Real fruit that lasts does not happen overnight. It is a continued walk with God. Busyness is not necessarily fruit bearing. Activities do not please God, fruit pleases God.

Roman 7:4

Therefore, my brethren, you also were made to die to the Law through the body of Christ, so that you might be joined to another, to Him who was raised from the dead, in order that we might bear fruit for God.

Prior to Jesus, your only way to bear fruit in the Kingdom was to fulfill the law. As long as you fulfilled the law, dotted your i's and crossed your t's, you were considered fruitfulness. What happened was, you were married to the law in order to have a "baby," which is your fruitfulness. Scripture says, "The only way we can be set free from the law is death." (Romans 7:6). Because you were guilty, Jesus died to make you free. Because of your New Testament marriage, you must bring forth your fruit. When two people get married, they produce fruit! Jesus and you must produce Kingdom fruit.

Too often we think that salvation is the end, rather than understand that salvation is merely the opening act. You have to be saved to enter into the Kingdom. That is your admission ticket. It gets you in the door. Once you are in the door, you have to get to the activities inside. That means you have to find your gifts and calling. You have to learn what God created you to do. You have to learn what sphere of influence God has put you on the earth to inhabit. You have to learn how to be the best in your particular area.

You do not have time to sit and enjoy Heaven yet! First of all, you are not yet in Heaven, you merely have the ticket to get through the door. While you are waiting for your Heavenly entrance, you must be about the Father's business. You must not be so Heavenly minded that you are no earthly good. You are called to inhabit the promised land. It is your gift, but it is not a land given to you. You must fight for it. You must better yourself, study your sphere of influence, know more than any other person in that sphere, and then step into the sphere and work your way up, if need be. There are no short cuts. You must work diligently and honestly. You cannot trick your way to the top. It is only through fulfilling your calling that you can become the man and woman of God that you were created to be – created to be before you were in the womb.

8. Whoever you are married to, you will bear the fruit of.

If you want to see who you are abiding in, check your fruit. Some of you have married the church when you are supposed to be married to Jesus to bring forth the fruit of the Kingdom. What are the fruits of the Kingdom?

You bear fruit by affirming the Kingdom of God through teaching, preaching, performing miracles, casting out demons, and being a witness. That is how you affirm the Kingdom of God on the earth. If I cast out demons by the finger of God, then Jesus said the Kingdom of God has come to you. That is the affirmation of the Kingdom of God.

You bear fruit through a Godly lifestyle, calling, and ministry.

Matthew 5:16

Let your light shine before men in such a way that they may see your good works, and glorify your Father who is in Heaven.

Let them see what? You good ideas? Your good looks? Your good church attendance? Do not tell me there is no responsibility to work around here. In this Kingdom, you work! You work for the Kingdom of God to bring forth fruit. If you do not work, they cannot see your works or God.

Luke 13:6-9

And He began telling this parable: "A man had a fig tree which had been planted in the vineyard; and he came looking for fruit on it and did not find any. And he said to the vineyard keeper, 'Behold, for three years I have come looking for fruit on this fig tree without finding any. Cut it down! Why does it even use up the ground?' and he answered and said to him. 'Let it alone, sir, for this year too, until I dig around it and put in fertilizer and if it bears fruit next year, fine, but if not, cut it down.'"

The fig tree did not produce fruit, so it was cut down. Jesus was hungry and went to the fig tree and was hungry, but it bore no fruit. The barren fig tree so displeased Jesus that He declared over it that it would never bear fruit again. Fruitfulness is a high priority for God.

Living the lifestyle of the Kingdom of God and proving you are the image of God is extremely important.

Galatians 5:22-23

But the fruit of the Spirit is love, joy, peace, patience, kindness, goodness, faithfulness, gentleness, self-control; against such things there is no law.

The fruit of the Spirit is the image of God. You are to project the image of God. Just like you see the image of God, it is not with visible sight that you see God. You see God in the love of a husband for his wife. You see God in the hand reaching out to the feed the hungry. You see God in the giving of money to better the life of others. You see God in giving up something dear to you for the sake of someone else without thought of gifts in return.

All of these, and more, are ways to see an invisible God in a visible world. You have heard that you are the only Jesus that some people will ever see. That is exactly what we are talking about here. Being Jesus so that others can see Jesus, that they might believe in Jesus, and ultimately become Jesus to someone else. That is how the Kingdom is supposed to work. It was never designed to be a Kingdom of Sunday morning, Sunday night, and Wednesday night only. It was always designed to be a Kingdom that occupied every minute of every day.

Activation Points:

1. Why is producing fruit so important in the Kingdom of God?

2. Explain the following statements:

    A) It is better "to not have had" the Kingdom of God than "to have had it and lost it."

    B) The requirement of your citizenship in the Kingdom of God is to bring forth fruit from it.

    C) The demand of the Kingdom of God is either 100% or no commitment at all.

    D) Church attendance alone is not commitment to the Kingdom of God.

SECTION THREE:

UNDERSTANDING GROWTH AND RESULTS

CHAPTER ELEVEN:
THE POWER OF ONE

The Power of One – What is the significance of one person? In our logical minds we think in terms of more people equals more power. **We think that quantity dictates accomplishment but in actuality, what will trump quantity every time is quality.** Therefore, one quality person is greater than many in quantity who are weak in the things of the Kingdom.

There are many situations that one person cannot handle alone. We live in a culture that says things like, "There is no I in team." It seems like the calls for unity (in many cases uniformity) and the value of the group over the individual are growing louder and louder across the world. Much of the world is built on the culture of the community where community is viewed as more important than individualism. And there is no doubt that there are times in history where the communal idea or the mass protest and movement won the day. There are, however, also history makers who stood as individuals who significantly altered the course of our world forever. North America was founded by pioneers who left everything to come here. As a result of this, many of us believe in the value of the individual. The belief in the individual is waning in North America, however, as there are more and more cries for diversity and acceptance.

There is also the African worldview that it takes a village. There is, after all, a certain safety in numbers. All of these concepts lead us to believe that quantity is as important, if not more important, than quality.

The same is not true in the spiritual realm. That is what we are talking about here. **To some degree quality is a forgotten art;**

we live in a world that mass produces everything. The first one looks like the last one, there is nothing to differentiate or distinguish one from the other. Remember the story of Gideon, where God continually narrowed down the number of soldiers that were available to fight the coming battle (Judges 7:2-7).

Likewise, Elijah saw that he did not need an army to fight the battle because he saw into the spiritual realm and realized that "those with us are greater than those against us." (2 Kings 6:16). All of this works into understanding that quality will always matter more than quantity.

The church needs to rid itself of the temptation to think that our solution is found in numbers, or the idea that if we can just get everyone "on the same page," God will "move." Jesus changed the world, for over two thousand years now, by speaking directly into the lives of twelve men. And one of them was Judas, who betrayed Him.

When it comes to the Kingdom of God, one is a majority. Because of the nature of covenant, we understand this. Covenant essentially means that what is mine is yours and what is yours is mine. When you have a covenant with God you should have access to all that is His, and He, or course, has access to all that is you.

This is what gave David an audacity, an unbelievable boldness, to walk out before a giant. This giant was bigger than him. The armies of the Philistines were there. In those days the Philistines were some of the most grotesque people of the known world. And here was David facing a giant. David rejected Saul's armor, walked out there, and looked up at this huge giant. On top of all of that, Goliath was cursing him by the names of his gods.

For David to have that boldness was amazing. He faced this giant and while Goliath was cursing him, literally words backed up by witchcraft and sorcery. He was cursing David and Israel by the name of his demon gods. Of course we know David had previously spoke of Goliath, not with curse words, but referred to him as, "uncircumcised" (1Samuel 17:26,43).

David was literally facing one of the fiercest warriors in the world. Seasoned veterans of the Israeli army were afraid to even look on the battle field where Goliath stood taunting God and God's army. David was the least likely warrior in Israel. He had no training. He had no armor. He had no weapon, except for a shepherd's sling, not designed to fight giants, but designed to scare off animals that might attack a sheep that is grazing.

In spite of everything that said walk away, leave the fight to the trained soldiers, David could not, because he was such a fierce servant of God. He was the "one." He was so wrapped up in his zeal for the God of his fathers that he did not even hesitate to step up and answer the challenge.

He was taken to King Saul, who was taller than other men and the fiercest warrior in the country. Now, imagine that Saul was not impressed. He probably wondered who this runt was who thinks he is qualified to take on a giant. Saul knew that, if he sent David to fight his fight and David was defeated, Saul and his army would be humiliated and likely defeated. David could easily have become the rallying cry for the Philistine army as they charged across the field to destroy the army of Israel.

David had an uphill battle. He had to convince his King that he was prepared for the fight. That was exactly what David did. How did he do it? He called on his passion to destroy anyone who would slander the name of his God. He had to present such a great force that Saul must have believed that David could win the battle. So, Saul let David go to battle, with only his sling and five smooth stones.

So, David faced the "uncircumcised" giant. David's verbal assault on Goliath seems meaningless if you don't understand the power of covenant. While face to face on the battlefield, David called Goliath an "uncircumcised Philistine." Why was that such a smite at Goliath? It meant, "Goliath, you have no covenant with the Almighty God and I do. Therefore, no matter what my stature is, I am a majority! Because, what is God's is mine, and you do not have a covenant with God." On that basis, we see the power of one.

The Bible says that the Heavens are the Lord's and the earth has been given to the sons of men. Since God operates in legalities, for God to do anything great in the earthly dimension, under the sun, He needs to find someone. He must find somebody to get the job done. In fact, the New Testament says the people marveled that God would give such authority to men. While the people's thoughts and marvels were focused on a single man Jesus, notice that Scripture says plural "men" not singular "man." They marveled that God would entrust such powerful authority to heal the sick, to cast out demons, literally to usher in the Kingdom of God to the earth. They marveled that God would give this authority, the legal right, to all of mankind. The people were astonished by this.

This is the beauty of how God has chosen to work on the earth. **He is actually looking for people to step up and be the one.** He longs for His children to take their rightful place as sons, heirs, and conquerors. This is not some trite saying; it is the Truth. God is ready to support you as you stand like David and refuse to allow the name of God to be mocked. He is ready to support you as you stand in city hall and bring honesty and integrity to city government. He is ready to support you when you start reaching out to addicts and the homeless to restore them to a life worthy of the calling of God in their lives.

God is not hiding from you. He is seeking you out. He knows who you are. He knows your gifts and calling. He knows your inadequacies. None of these things can prevent you from fulfilling your calling when you become a majority of one in God's Kingdom!

Isaiah 6:8

Then I heard the voice of the Lord, saying, "Whom shall I send and who will go for us?" Then I said, "Here am I. Send me!"

When God wants to do something on earth, He looks for someone. The spirit of socialism that resides in Canadian Church culture, especially opposes apostles (planters and culture changers) and prophets (perceivers of Truth), reduces leaders down to the generic concept that we cannot do anything without unity. Or it reduces everything to the concept that we have to be completely unified for God to move. That simply is not Biblical.

Does unity access and invite blessing in the Kingdom of God? Absolutely! Where there is unity there is a commanded blessing. **There is revival where there is unity.** It is good for brothers to dwell together in unity. If God calls you to be "the one" this does not mean you should break the bond of peace or unity – or walk in dishonor. God can use one, because one is a majority by the standards of the Kingdom of God.

Principle number one is this, if righteous ones are silent, then evil will reign. Even God is "helpless" where Christians are passive. Edmund Burke, the great British statesman, is often quoted about one particular statement he made. He said, "All that is necessary for evil to triumph is for good men to do nothing." Albert Einstein understood this principle. In fact, he summed it up well when he said, "The world is a dangerous place to live; not because of the people who are evil, but because of the people who don't do anything about it." Albert said this as he lived through the birth of Nazi Germany. He witnessed a lot of good people doing nothing because they were afraid, because they did not think they could make a difference. **If**

righteous ones remain silent then evil reigns. Even God is helpless where Christians are passive.

Principle number two is this, Jesus actually did not use a mob of people to change the world. He used twelve "ones." He taught each "one" to do what He did; that is, 12 separate individuals to be like Him, who eventually went 12 separate ways into 12 different parts of the then-known world. Jesus was the one. He was the man! His ability to be a majority was founded in reproducing what made Himself great into 12 other ones. In fact, He related differently with those 12 than He did with the seventy. He related differently with the three, Peter, James, and John, than He did with the twelve. He related to Peter and to John differently than He did with the others.

Jesus understands the value of one.

We have to get a grasp of this principle. Without it we will flounder around, never accomplishing anything for the Kingdom of God. We will spend our lives waiting on someone to answer the call, all while God is waiting on us to answer the call. God has prepared the way. He has given you everything you need to be successful. You still have to step out of the boat, often at the most fearful time, to walk on the water. It takes great faith, great confidence, but what a testimony – I am walking on water.

Jesus dealt with the twelve disciples with pressure, intensity, correction, and discipline. He rebuked them, scolded them, pushed them, and even commanded one of them to get out of a boat during a fierce storm. That is how Jesus developed those ones. **Pressure and intensity develops the ones. It brings the cream to the surface.**

Sometimes, when we have an overemphasis on corporate authority based upon unity, we actually can create a culture where everyone believes someone else will do it. We think that once we have worked hard enough to create unity, then God will be the one, because our unity has pleased God. We think, "Now He will be the one to solve all of our nation's problems!" All the while, God is saying, "I am just trying to find one."

The Bible says that nations were delivered by one, by a prophet the Lord delivered Israel (Hosea 12:13). A whole nation was delivered by Moses; Moses was the one.

Be the one and others will follow your example. In God's Kingdom, it is absolutely inappropriate to see yourself as irrelevant. It is the sin of irresponsibility to minimize yourself as a potential steward of the Kingdom of God. That is because in the Kingdom of God, it just takes one. You are defacing and insulting the blood of Jesus when you minimize your own potential.

David was found in a field. He was not even numbered with his brothers. He was not even included as a potential one in the lineup. Yet, he turned out to be the one.

It is the same for you. You might consider yourself the least likely person and think you could never make a difference. But if you believe that, it is because you do not understand that you plus God is a majority. He created you to be alive right now. He chose you to understand this teaching, He chose you to change the sphere of influence where He called you. Do not be satisfied to go through life waiting on some other one. Be the one! Do not walk through life in a dream. Live the dream! Do not wander through your wilderness feeling lost and alone. Connect with God! Find your calling! Learn what your gifts are! They are there. They might be hidden, but they are there. You only have one job – find your calling and learn your gifts. Then, use them to the glory of the Kingdom of God!

2 Chronicles 16:9

"For the eyes of the Lord move to and fro throughout the earth that He may strongly support those whose heart is completely His. You have acted foolishly in this. Indeed, from now on you will surely have wars."

There is great potential within one single seed. The Bible says that the eyes of the Lord look to and fro over the earth seeking somebody, seeking a one, even one person whom He can show Himself powerful on their behalf. The eyes of the Lord would not be looking to and fro if He was looking for a majority (2 Chronicles 16:9). He is looking for one. He is looking for someone.

When you choose to be the one, religious people often call it "youthful zeal." Or they call it arrogance. They do not realize that, you believe in yourself because you know, with God you are a majority. If God be for me, who can be against me. Be the one.

We see this in I Samuel 17:26-32.

I Samuel 17:26-32

Then David spoke to the men who were standing by him, saying, "What will be done for the man who kills this Philistine and takes away the reproach from Israel? For who is this uncircumcised Philistine, that he should taunt the armies of the living God?" The people answered him in accord with this word, saying, "This it will be done to the man who kills him." Now, Eliab, his oldest brother heard what he spoke to the men; and Eliab's anger burned against David and he said, "Why have you come down? And with whom have you left those few sheep in the wilderness? I know your insolence and the wickedness of your heart; for you have come down in order to see the battle." But David said, "What have I done now? Was it not just a question?" Then he turned away from him to another and said the same thing; and the people answered the same thing as before. When the words which David spoke were heard, they told them to Saul, and he sent for him. David said to Saul, "Let no man's heart fail because of him; your servant will go and fight with this Philistine."

This is the little shepherd boy, who brought "cheese and crackers and sausage to the party." Eliab says that he knows the evil of David's heart. When God begins to use you, it is very possible that some of the people closest to you will take offense, and even falsely accuse you, or question your motives.

The local church of today should be a breeding ground of those who choose to be the one. I became frustrated with the local church not being a breeding ground for ones. So I created the History Makers Society, which is somewhat of a church without walls, comprised of people who are saying, "I will be the one."

William Wilberforce was one. He was in the British House of Commons and reached a crossroads between formal ministry and politics. He remained a Member of Parliament and singlehandedly lead the charge to end the slave trade in the British Empire, making slavery illegal. He challenged an empire, at the height of its power. He was one.

Mother Teresa, a young girl, probably in her early teens, felt called to go to India, despite her superiors recommending against it. She was persistent. She went to India with nothing and started helping those who were starving. She chose to become the one. She literally was the one for India in the history books. Now this simple nun is known and respected the world over, not for being great, but for refusing to let us ignore the least amongst us. You want to talk about a life well-lived, she is it!

Joan of Arc was also very young. She singlehandedly turned the armies of Britain away from France and reestablished governmental order in France. She had never before wielded a sword or ridden a horse. She started having encounters with God. She had no family support. Very few were for her because she was a woman. In fact, her own people harbored such jealousy against her that they basically gave her up to be martyred. That is wild! It was the price of being the one. She stood in the gap alone, with only God beside her. She is still talked about because she lived a life worth living. She was "one of the ones" that Hebrews says are people of whom the world was not worthy.

Anyone can be the one, if they are willing to pay the price.

Activation Points:

1. Identify your place of influence and calling.

2. Ask the Lord for His vision and dream for that sphere of calling.

3. Develop a strategy of how to begin influencing that sphere.

4. Be the one and start doing in that sphere what others are not doing.

CHAPTER TWELVE:

THE POWER OF ONE GOOD SEED

Whenever God wants to do something big, He starts with something small. In fact, whenever God wants to do something big, He starts with someone small. God understands the power of incremental process. God understands how to do something big. When God does something significant, He always starts with someone insignificant. These are the principles by which He works. Probably because He gets the glory. Probably because too much too fast is never good.

God chooses to use people to set up His Kingdom on the earth. He could easily do it Himself, after all, He created the whole thing. Yet, in spite of God's awesome abilities, He chooses to use you and me. It is in the Kingdom DNA that God established before the very foundations of the world. It is why He sent Jesus to redeem us from the curse and help us grow to the point of maturity.

Anything that is to last a long time and have progressive increase, must start small. Even Israel, when they were taking over the Promised Land, was given the Promised Land in increments. We understand it was so that the culture of the world would not subdue their culture.

God understands that growing in wisdom and knowledge is a process. He knows that no one person is born understanding the secrets of the Universe or His Kingdom. God knows we need each other. God knows that we are fallen creatures in this world before He redeems us. All of this helps us understand how God works with man. With all of our shortcomings, He works with us.

When God gave the first commission to mankind in Genesis 1:27-28, His goal was to fill the earth and subdue it. We have never found the geographical location of the Garden of Eden. We think we know where it might have been, somewhere in present-day Iraq, but we have never actually found it. I believe the Garden of Eden was a concentrated location, a replica of Heaven. A concentrated place of God's glory on earth. It was like a seed of Heaven, placed on the earth.

Genesis 1:27-28

God created man in His own image, in the image of God He created him; male and female He created them. God blessed them; and God said to them, "Be fruitful and multiply, and fill the earth, and subdue it; and rule over the fish of the sea and over the birds of the sky and over every living thing that moves on the earth."

God was not merely interested in people filling the earth and multiplying. He wanted people after His own image and likeness to fill the earth, multiply, and subdue it. I believe that God wanted men and women to carry the glory of God and spread out over the earth beyond the Garden. Glory carriers covering the earth! This was God's dream.

So "God created man in His own image, in the image of God He created him, male and female He created them. God blessed them. God said, "Be fruitful, multiply, fill the earth, and subdue it."

Remember, God is not impressed with quantity. God is always looking for quality. I believe God would rather have one man, one woman, or a small group of men and women working on His behalf, if they are filled with passion and zeal, than a large group of people half working, and consumed with their own needs and wants.

Gideon is a great example of this. The story is told in Judges 7. Gideon wanted a grand army because he was facing an incredibly superior force. Logic, the laws of war, the laws of physics, and all of these suggested that the only hope for the battle was to field the largest force he could find. God had other plans. God kept narrowing down the numbers until Gideon's more than 30,000 men were merely 300 (Judges 7:2-7).

Imagine standing over your army of 300 men, after you had started with over 30,000, looking at them as you prepare for a great battle. It does not inspire confidence. Instead, it tells you that there is only one way to win the coming battle. That way is God's way! There is only one King who can lead the troops and that King is God. It is at this point that you have to believe in the power of the one good seed. It is this point that you have to believe in the power of one. You have to see the world as God sees the world to take the step toward the battlefield, when all around you is telling you that there is no hope for you to win in your own strength.

These are the kinds of people that God is looking for. He is looking for people who serve Him, people who believe in Him, people who will rush forward into the fray without fear, because they know that God is the great deliverer.

God's strategy, or methodology for global domination was to start with two seeds – Adam and Eve. Actually it all began with Adam, a single good seed. God blessed Adam and Eve to take the glory, that was concentrated in the Garden of Eden, beyond the Garden and fill the earth and subdue it with the principles and the spirit of the Kingdom of God, the glory of God. That is why the Bible says, "The knowledge of the glory of God will cover the earth as the waters cover the seas."

So Adam and Eve began to be fruitful and multiply. They were filling the earth with God's dream of the earth being covered with the knowledge of the glory of God. The dream had begun. When Satan wanted to destroy it, he just had to corrupt the seed. He just had to introduce sin.

Satan does not have to take you all the way to hell to win the battle. He merely has to cause you to take your eyes off of God's plan. You see, it does not take the total destruction of the plan, it just takes you stepping to the side, and stopping moving forward. Sometimes the greatest method of Satan is to give us something good to replace what great thing God has. If he can keep us from reaching our full potential, he has won the battle.

In the days of Noah, the seed had become so corrupted that there were even fallen angels coming down and producing giants (Genesis 6:2-4). So when God wanted to start over again, He did not start from nothing, he began with Noah and his family. A few good seeds. If I was God, I would not have done it this way! If I had power to create human beings, I would have just created enough of them to fill the earth immediately! But our God understands the power of process. He has a strategy. He has a desire to empower us to reproduce after our own kind!

In fact, this is what He did in Genesis. He created everything once. Then, He subjected it to a system of reproduction after its kind. It is amazing. **God is the ultimate CEO.** Now, He does this again. He says, in Genesis 6:3, "Should I strive with man forever? His days are going to be 120 years."

I would have wiped out everybody. I would have started again with a second Adam. Instead, God saves a single seed, and seven other high quality seeds – Noah, his family. He puts them in a boat to protect the DNA, to protect the seed, and then He starts again. Through a few insignificant people, God is going to do something significant.

God actually reduces the number of people on the earth down to eight people. Eight being the number of new beginnings. This is called the Noahic Covenant. The covenant God made with Adam to be fruitful and fill the earth was called the Adamic Covenant. Now He makes a Noahic Covenant and says to Noah and his family, "You be fruitful and multiply, increase greatly on the earth. Multiply in it." (Genesis 9:1). Literally, all nations and all of us from that point on, have come through the line of Noah, one high quality seed, one righteous man.

For the second time, God commands a man and his family to be fruitful and multiply on the earth. God again uses the principle of one good seed to replenish the earth. He again gives man the authority to rule the earth. God is the God of second chances. He is giving man a second chance through another choice seed. He is showing His mercy to mankind, again.

Next comes the Abrahamic Covenant found in Genesis.

Genesis 15:1-5

After these things the word of the Lord came to Abram in a vision, saying, "Do not fear. Abram. I am a shield to you; your reward shall be very great." Abram said, "O Lord God, what will You give me, since I am childless, and the heir of my house is Eliezer of Damascus?" And Abram said, "Since You have given no offspring to me, one born in my house is my heir." Then behold, the word of the Lord came to him saying, "This man will not be your heir; but one who will come forth from your own body, he shall be your heir." And He took him outside and said, "Now look toward the Heavens, and count the stars, if you are able to count them." And He said to him, "So shall your descendants be."

God in now going to do something special for the world. He is going to do it through a single good seed. He chooses Abraham, after the Word of the Lord came to Abraham in a vision. Abraham says, "I am childless." This is the way we all are inclined to respond to God. Too often God wants to tell us a significant thing He wants to do through our insignificant selves, and we tell Him that it cannot happen. We forget the only thing that grows is Kingdom DNA. It is not about you. If God can put Kingdom DNA in you, nothing is impossible. So, Abraham expressed his lack of faith, but God declared that his offspring would be greater than the number of stars he could see. That is wild! "Number the stars if you are able, so shall the number of your offspring be." Out of one man, God Almighty is promising you will have descendants like the stars in the sky. God is actually speaking in irony, because He says to Abraham, "If you can number them." What is so amazing is that God knows Abraham cannot number them. In fact, it has been thousands of years since then and we still cannot number the amount of stars in the Universe. So shall your offspring be.

Later on God shows Abraham the sand on the seashore (Genesis 22:17). He says, "This is the number of your offspring. If you can count the sand." I could go down to a beach, scoop up a bucket of sand, it is probably billions of grains. (A cup is about 6-7 million grains of sand.) God says to Abraham your offspring is going to be like the sands on the seashore of the world. Are you serious? There is not enough room even on the globe to hold that many people.

Even as a child I can remember thinking that this would be impossible? I wondered what God meant by this. Here are three possibilities:

Number one: **God could be speaking in hyperbole.** It is just exaggerative language to get a point across. It could be. God could be making His point that He can do anything He wants, in regard to Abraham and his descendants. God is saying, "I can make your descendants as many as I want. Trust me. I can do everything!" This is a message that God wants us all to understand. He made the whole Universe; therefore, He can do anything He wants. What He wants to do is support us as we fulfill our calling, using the gifts He has placed in each of us. It really is that simple.

Number two: **It could be that God is speaking generationally.** Generational means that God is not referring to the amount of people on the planet at once, but He is speaking about generation after generation. That could lead us to believe that we are not seeing the end of time yet, for quite a while. Some people say that Jesus is not coming back as soon as we might think. We know that God does not lie. We know that by His very nature God always speaks the truth. If this is the case, then we need to continue to look forward.

Number Three: **God could be referring to Kingdom influence and Kingdom fruitfulness, which really cannot be counted.** When God moves, it is beyond the comprehension of man. It may be healing the sick, which defies logic and medicine. It may be setting free the captives from addictions that consume a man. It may be feeding the hungry, which is never as easy as it sounds because hunger occurs several times a day in each of us. Any of these works of God defy logic because we are trapped in time and space and cannot understand a God that lives outside of time and space. It is a mystery that will only be answered when we see Him face to face.

The stars in the sky and the sand on the seashore cannot be counted. God says, "Kings will come from you, Abraham. Whole nations will come from you." This is fascinating! All of this can come from a single, high quality seed like Father Abraham.

My great grandfather used to pray and intercede for every generation to come after him. So even before I was born, he was praying for me. That influence is still taking place. That is credited to him as fruitfulness. For example, there was a time when I was leading a revival meeting. I came home from this

143

meeting and I was feeling pretty good about myself. The service went really well; I was feeling like I was the anointed man! I was marveling with God at how He was using me. I remember the Lord interrupted my arrogant thinking, and He said, "Tonight had nothing to do with you! I was just honoring the prayers of your great-grandfather."

There is a lesson for each of us here. As God begins to use you, it is easy to get excited about the gifts that He has given you. It is easy to believe that the gifts are yours, not from God necessarily. This is a dangerous place to be!

Can you know what and how your life is affecting people, fruitfulness-wise? You cannot know it and you cannot count it. Picture Abraham attempting to count the stars. He could not, and you cannot. Count your influence if you can. You cannot! My great-grandfather could not possibly count that he would pray for a great-grandson who was at one time backslidden. Now look at all the things being done around the world through our History Makers Trainings. They are all credited back to great-grandfather's fruitfulness.

You cannot count your influence. I would fight an ongoing spiritual battle when I was preaching to 200 young adults. The devil would attack me on a Friday afternoon before going to that service. I would think, "I am only preaching to a couple of hundred people, we had a good service, and no one had gotten saved." The devil was attacking me like that? Why would he? Because the devil understands influence. He knew that maybe I would say something of Kingdom significance and one person would grab it. They would live it, they would teach it to their kids, and to their kids. He knew that would bring some kind of divine, high quality Kingdom DNA, and their family line would one day produce another Reinhard Bonnke or Billy Graham!

You cannot count the stars! In looking at how a seed functions; that is, the seed's ability to produce, you will see something amazing. You will see that inside a seed is a whole forest. Inside that forest are many seeds that have many forests. In the process of a seed becoming fruitful, it has to die. It has to go into the ground and pay the price in the hidden, unseen place. If a seed falls to the ground and dies, it will bring forth much fruit. The fruit begins based on what is happening underground in that seed. If the seed has Kingdom DNA, an orange tree can say it is an apple tree, but saying so does not change its nature. Suppose you have an orange seed and an apple seed, and you do not know which is which, test the DNA. Test the DNA and you will find out what linage that seed comes from.

Jesus taught a string of parables that are really crucial to this concept. God just needs a single seed that is willing to pay the price.

Matthew 13:3-8

And He spoke many things to them in parables, saying, "Behold, the sower went out to sow; and as he sowed, some seeds fell beside the road, and the birds came and ate them up. Others fell on rocky places, where they did not have much soil; and immediately they sprang up, because they had no depth of soil. But when the sun had risen, they were scorched; and because they had no root, they withered away. Others fell among the thorns, and the thorns came up and choked them out. And others fell on the good soil and yielded a crop, some a hundredfold, some sixty, and some thirty."

This is called the parable of the sower. This parable is all about the soil. The ability to produce in this story is not necessarily based on the quality of the seed, but the quality of the soil.

The reason why this is such a good passage for what we are talking about, is because we actually get a quantifiable number of what a single good seed can produce. **In God's eyes, a seed can produce a hundredfold, sixtyfold, or thirtyfold.** Thank you Jesus for telling us that this is what we can expect. Many pastors only fix their eyes on how many people are in their services, when God is thinking of Kingdom influence! Jesus is saying that you can actually produce a hundredfold. At that point, the disciples only know that He is talking about the Word preached, the Gospel of Salvation. The soil is the hearts of the people. Jesus, however, took the parable a little deeper later on.

Matthew 13:24-30

Jesus presented another parable to them, saying, "The kingdom of Heaven may be compared to a man who sowed good seed in his field. But while his men were sleeping, his enemy came and sowed tares among the wheat, and went away. But when the wheat sprouted and bore grain, then the tares became evident also. The slaves of the landowner came and said to him, 'Sir, did you not sow good seed in your field? How then does it have tares?' And he said to them 'An enemy has done this!' The slaves said to him, 'Do you want us, then, to go and gather them up?' But he said, 'No; for while you are gathering up the tares, you may uproot the wheat with them. Allow both to grow together until the harvest; and in the time of the harvest I will say to the reapers. 'First gather up the tares and bind them in bundles to burn them up; but gather the wheat into my barn.'"

When we jump into Matthew 13:24, this is called the parable of the weeds. In the parable of the weeds Jesus throws a curve ball. This is where the seeds are compared to the weeds and the seeds are no longer just the Word of God preached, **these seeds are now people.** Now people have a potential, a hundredfold, sixtyfold, thirtyfold. Jesus goes on to compare and try to draw a picture of the Kingdom of God and the power of Kingdom DNA.

Matthew 13:31-32

He presented another parable to them, saying, "The kingdom of Heaven is like a mustard seed, which a man took and sowed in

146

his field; and this is smaller than all other seeds, but when it is full grown, it is larger than the garden plants and becomes a tree, so that THE BIRDS OF THE AIR COME and NEST IN ITS BRANCHES."

In Matthew 13:31 this is called the parable of the mustard seed. It is a great example of how God uses the laws of nature and the Universe to produce great things from insignificant things. Looking at the mustard seed one would assume that not much would come from it. God, however, has other plans. **He often hides His greatest work in the least likely places.** He often hides His greatest work in a person who has no natural gifts, but a great belief in God's ability to bring forth His will through a vessel willing to submit to the working of God in his life. It is yet another great example of God growing something insignificant into something significant!

Matthew 13:33

He spoke another parable to them. "The kingdom of Heaven is like leaven, which a woman took and hid in three pecks of flour until all was leavened."

This is called the parable of the leaven. This one is really great. The parable is simply about how the leaven expands and takes over. Just like what God wanted to have happen for Adam, Noah, Abraham, and even you and me. Now Jesus also tries to compare the finished product, which is the Kingdom of Heaven. He is saying, "How can I illustrate the greatness of this Kingdom? How can I illustrate the take-over potential of this Kingdom, the magnitude of the Kingdom of God? How can I explain to these earthlings the magnitude of My Kingdom?" Even how the Kingdom functions, how it works, how you get it. It is invisible, and yet it is real. How can Jesus describe this Kingdom?

In the parable of the mustard seed, Jesus says, "Actually, the Kingdom of God, the best way I could describe it, is like the tiniest of all seeds. It is a seemingly insignificant seed." As Jesus is describing this, you can imagine the puzzled look on the faces of the disciples. He is saying the Kingdom of God is like the tiniest of seeds, but He does not stop there. He says, "That seed grows and it becomes not only a great tree, but it becomes the greatest of trees. That tree actually becomes so influential and so great, that it is greater than all of the other garden plants because of its DNA." It is truly Kingdom DNA. It stretches out its branches into society. The birds of the air come and nest in its shade. The beasts of the field come and lay down under it. This tree becomes the influential tree.

What is really fascinating about this is that when Jesus is describing the Kingdom of God, He does not just describe it as the tiniest of seeds. He does not just describe it in its finished product as a tree. He describes the Kingdom of God as a PROCESS from small to great. That is His best way of painting a picture of how the Kingdom of God works. The Kingdom of God is like leaven, starting small and then taking over. The Kingdom of God is like a tiny seed starting small and then taking over.

If it is truly Kingdom DNA, no matter how small you start, you will become great. No matter how small you begin, no matter how insignificant you are; in fact, the more insignificant you are, the greater the Kingdom effect when it begins to grow you and increase you.

Now the disciples are confused and they take Jesus aside.

Matthew 13:36-39

Then He left the crowds and went into the house. And His disciples came to Him and said, "Explain to us the parable of the tares of the field." And He said, "The one who sows the good seed is the Son of Man, and the field is the world; and as for the good seed, those are the sons of the kingdom; and the tares are the sons of the evil one; and the enemy who sowed them is the devil, and the harvest is the end of the age, and the reapers are angels."

Then the disciples say, "Jesus, we understood that You were talking about the Word preached, but now it sounds like You are saying that now we are the Word preached, we are the seed. What are You talking about, Jesus?" Now we come to the parable of the weeds explained.

At this point, Jesus explains to them that the good seeds are the "sons of the Kingdom." We are the seeds that are being sown into society for the purpose of bringing forth a harvest of fruit, some one-hundredfold, some sixtyfold, and some thirtyfold.

What is so significant about "fold?"

What is so fascinating about fold is that fold is not multiplication. We typically think that "fold" means 30 times, 60 times, or 100 times. Most Christian leaders can't imagine 100-fold fruitfulness, so we interpret what Jesus was saying as mere multiplication. Ah, but remember, He is the God of Abraham who promised him fruit and results like the stars in the sky and the sand on the seashore!

We must learn to see everything through God's eyes. God's eyes are like a telescope and a microscope all in one. They see everything, from the smallest detail to the largest picture. They see all the way to the single atom and beyond. They see all the way to the edge of the Universe and beyond. When we learn to see as God sees we will change how we approach the world. It will change how we approach people. It will change how we approach situations that would normally overwhelm us. **Everything changes when we learn to view the world through God's eyes!**

When you get into what fold means, the principle of folds is actually compounding doubles. Compounding doubles is like this: you have one seed, one fold, think of a piece of paper that is literally folded once in half, now you have two. Two fold, now you have four. Three fold, you do not have six, you have eight. Each time you fold, the number is doubled from the fold before.

Thirtyfold is the guy who does not do much, the guy on the low end. He did what he could. He was faithful with little. Yet thirtyfold is actually 1,073,701,824. That is one billion, seventy-three million, seven hundred and one thousand, eight hundred and twenty-four.

Wow! Now, that is not the number of the sand on the seashore or the stars in the sky, but that is God's scale.

We are trying to bring somebody out to the church barbeque. We do not even know the effect we are having. So you are reading this right now, and I am not thinking about just one. I think if you can catch something right now we can lead many sons to glory through your genealogy and lineage.

What will you attach your faith to? Abraham needed faith because these kinds of numbers can only be done by grace through faith.

We must come to be like the heroes of the faith who are talked about in Hebrews 11. Many of them died never having received or physically seen the promise. They did not, however, waiver in their belief that God was faithful to do what He had promised. So, they died in faith, knowing that God is not bound by the life of a man or a woman. He is only bound by His Word. He is faithful and His Word will not return to Him void; it will accomplish what He desires it to accomplish.

Sixtyfold, you would think, is thirty fold doubled, however, it is not!

Instead it is 1,151,973,021,073,889,216, one quintillion, one hundred and fifty-one quadrillion, nine hundred and seventy-three trillion, twenty-one billion, seventy-three million, eight hundred and eighty-nine thousand, two hundred and sixteen.

Imagine how valuable each person is to God and His Kingdom! Maybe you sat beside an older gentleman in church for years and assumed he was insignificant. Maybe he attended church for years, sat in the same place, and had never led anyone to the Lord. He appeared insignificant. Then, he went through the process the seed has to go through, that was in the form of History Makers Training, and the Transformation Council Curriculum. Am I talking about a real person? Yes, this man actually exists. He now oversees three different senior's groups in different locations. He has created a program called "Budding with Seniors." He is now leading people to Christ regularly. They are now not just influencing the seniors, but they are also influencing the staff.

That is the power of a single good seed. If it is Kingdom DNA that person who was once seemingly insignificant becomes significant!

Let's now look at a hundredfold. That is 1,200,064,595,207,167,685,882,431,343,616. A number beyond imagination, one nonillion, two hundred octillion, sixty-four septillion, five hundred ninety-five sextillion, two hundred seven quintillion, one hundred sixty-seven quadrillion, six hundred eighty-five trillion, eight hundred and eighty-two billion, four hundred thirty-one million, three hundred forty-three thousand, six hundred and eighteen.

The best seed produces the greatest return. What does it take to be the best seed? Is it enough to be from a wealthy home? No!

Is it enough to be from a well-educated home? No! It has nothing to do with the measurements that men place on a person's value. It has to do with being willing to be used by God and go through the process of sonship. It has to do with being willing to die once you are planted in the ground, so that life can come from the death process. It has to do with a seed that is so in tune with God that Kingdom DNA is all that is left in that seed. The process is not an easy one. The outcome, however, is so beyond what we could ask or think that it is well worth the pain of the process. That is the power of a single good seed!

Activation Points:

1. "Whenever God wants to do something big, He starts with something small." Prove this statement by giving Scriptural examples.

2. What role does your faith play in producing fruit that is bigger than you ever imagined?

3. How has this chapter impacted your view of ministry and life?

4. According to Jesus, what amount of fruitfulness should we expect from a "good seed?"

5. Explain the statement, "It is not about the quality of the soil, but it is the quality of the seed."

CHAPTER THIRTEEN:
THE US FACTOR

We are going to start this chapter by looking at the book of Genesis. This is where we come to understand how God created everything. It is also where we see how He ordained man and woman to rule over the kingdom of this earth. Here we see God set everything that is set. Here we see God establish the rules of this dimension. **Here we see God establish His relationship with mankind.** And it is here we see man fall and be given a task less than what he was created for. The rest of the Bible shows us how God works to restore us to the place He has for us, a place where we hold dominion over the kingdom of earth and its inhabitants.

Genesis 11:1-4

Now, the whole earth used the same language and the same words. It came about as they journeyed east, that they found a plain in the land of Shinar and settled there. They said to one another, "Come, let us make bricks and burn them thoroughly." And they used bricks for stone, and they used tar for mortar. They said, "Come, let us build for ourselves a city and a tower whose top will reach into Heaven, and let us make for ourselves a name, otherwise we will be scattered abroad over the face of the whole earth."

Here we have a group of people banding together saying, "We're going to build ourselves a tower that will reach to Heaven. We are going to do a great thing." Listen to how the Scripture words it. It says in verse four, "They said come, let US, build for OURSELVES a city and a tower whose top will reach into

Heaven. **And let US make for OURSELVES a name."** (Emphasis added.)

What was happening here is a group of people wanted to band together collectively and have their little inner circle. They did not want to be scattered across the face of the earth, they wanted their own little community, in their own little confines, and they were building a great tower to Heaven – just for themselves. They were thinking, "This is the Tower of Babel and nobody gets in here but us. We are building a great tower so the world will look at us and marvel at the tower we have built for ourselves."

Notice that they did not want to be scattered abroad.

In God's economy, what does God want the church to do? **He wants His church to go everywhere, to cover the earth as water covers the seas, to scatter, and be fruitful and multiply.** He wanted them to subdue the earth, not just for themselves, but to see the world saved and the Kingdom come. This company of people had an anti-Kingdom mentality. Whenever you do something solely for yourself, you have become anti-Kingdom of God. I am talking about whenever you think only of yourself, you are thinking "Me, me, me, me." You are becoming anti-Kingdom of God because God called you to be fruitful, to multiply, and to reach many people.

Notice how many times the word "us" has been used in this passage of Scripture. The Holy Spirit was trying to give us a hint, a wink from God. He is saying that these people were selfish. These people wanted to build their own kingdom. These people wanted to do things just for themselves. The greatest enemy is "Us." When you think "self," no matter what you do in life, even if you are not fighting in a battle against the devil, you are fighting yourself. Say for example, God gives you a million dollars; now, you will become overly focused on yourself. This happens in more ways than just money. You may get into a new level of life at school, or a promotion at work. It is not necessarily the devil you have got to worry about, it becomes about "You or Us."

You take time away from God and begin to indulge yourself, you might not be fighting the devil, my friends, you might be fighting self. It is Us you need to worry about. God begins to bless a young adult ministry and they begin to have testimonies. They begin to do things. Great things are going on, and that is good, but they have to be mindful of the Us factor. Why do you need to be on guard or carefully concerned about yourself? Because it is possible for God to do something through you, and for you to take improper credit for it.

It is not always about an evil factor when Us is involved. Look at the first church in Jerusalem. In Acts 8, Stephen has just become the second martyr of the church, Jesus being the first. Saul, who was later converted and became known as Paul, was in hearty agreement with putting Stephen to death (Acts 22:20). It was a dark moment for the church because it was immediately obvious to everyone in church that the cost was going to be great.

Acts 8:1b

...And on that day a great persecution began against the church in Jerusalem, and they were all scattered throughout the regions of Judea and Samaria, except the apostles.

The early church, for whatever reason, was following the nature of man. They were sitting in Jerusalem. They were enjoying the newly created Christian Church and they were working directly with Jesus' disciples, the Apostles. They were growing and God was blessing them. Everything was going well except for that pesky Saul.

There was, however, a large problem. They were staying in one group. They were not going into all the world and making

155

disciples. They were staying in Jerusalem and making disciples. While it was great for the church to get started, for the church to become what Jesus had died to make it they would have to go further than Jerusalem.

Never fear, God had a way to see that His plan was fulfilled. He allowed persecution to arise. Saul came to Jerusalem, Stephen was killed, and a great persecution arose. It seems like a dark day in the history of the church.

It was not a dark day, however, because God is always in control – even when it seems that the world is spinning out of control! Just as He did with the village building the Tower of Babel, God used this persecution to scatter the church throughout the region.

God is not the God of bunch up and serve yourself. God is not the God of Us. God is the God who has called us to go into all the world and make disciples of the nations! What a great calling! What an honor to serve a God with such a broad, loving vision for every man, woman, and child on the earth.

Never forget, all of your accomplishments are the result of the Lord working through you. It is by grace. The enemy is Us. We want to build something for Us. This was the problem with these people. Let Us build a tower.

Ask yourself this question, "Am I willing to lose everything for the Lord? What am I willing to lose for God?" Truly the secret to life is: I do not own anything – that is the secret. If you do not own anything, you will never be disappointed when you lose something. If you do not own anything, then in your heart, when that thing is taken from you, it is not a big deal. Jesus is your portion because you do not own anything. In your heart, He is your reward, He is your everything. When you do not own anything and it becomes a great success, God can entrust you with it, because you do not own anything!

God can entrust success and fruitfulness to those who will not own it. I am not talking about do not pay attention to it or do not be a good steward of it. I am talking about your heart connecting with that thing, to the point where it becomes an idol in your life.

I am not talking about bad things, either. I am talking about good things. I am talking about houses that you need for protection from the elements. I am talking about cars that you need to get to your worship service where you worship, and to work. I am talking about jobs to supply the money to take care of your needs.

It would be easy if we were talking about bad or evil things. It would be easy not to own them. It would be easy to keep our hearts pure. The trouble comes when we are trying to keep our hearts pure over something that it is not wrong for us to use or have. That is when we most need to guard our hearts!

Lose everything already in your hearts, young people, and God will bless you with more. Lose it in your heart.

Unfortunately, the consequences of not surrendering in one area of life, can be incredibly devastating on everything that comes after it.

Lose everything already in your heart and let God become your treasure. *The degree that you can kill your flesh, is the degree that you will enjoy life.*

If I do not really own my money and if I lose it, it does not really hinder my ability to worship. It does not hinder my relationships. It does not hinder my time with God. Best of all, it does not steal my joy. If I do not own my house as a treasure in my heart and then if I lose my house, it does not matter. It does not matter what the economy is doing, because it is not mine. God has given to me what I have, to manage, and God can take it back whenever He wants to. I do not own it and when it is taken from me, my Christianity does not falter because I do not own anything.

The great thing about this is that you become immune to faltering when life's circumstances are bad. You are not moved by circumstances any more. Why? Because the only thing you own never fails and that is Jesus. The only thing you own is those times with God, your Bible, and the things in your heart between you and God that you hold dear. That is all you own.

No matter what comes your way, even sickness, you are OK in your heart. Of course we should never accept sickness without doing what we can to fight and overcome it. However, I have often thought that if I were in the hospital and was going to lose my life, I would go through great fear. I am sure I would go through a whole lot of emotions. I do not, however, own my life. To live is Christ, to die is gain (Philippians 1:21). So, even staring in the face of death, I do not own my life. I only own Him. He is my treasure and He is my success.

We really need to grasp this concept. You have heard the saying, "Everybody wants to go to Heaven, but nobody wants to die." That statement is true because we do not truly understand the basic concept of life and death. When we truly believe that to live is Christ and to die is gain we will be set free to live life to its fullest. When we truly believe that everything we have is a gift from God, we will be set free to own anything and not be consumed by it. When we truly believe that eternity matters more than anything that happens in the fleeting brevity of existence that we call life, we will be able to walk in the spirit realm, rather than the natural realm. That is what Jesus did. He knew that Heaven was more real than the earth. He knew that the earth is a mere shadow compared to Heaven. He knew that whatever He did on earth would only be relevant if it effected eternity.

We need this same approach to life. We need this same belief system so engrained in us that we barely see the world around us as it is. **We need to see the world around as it will be once Jesus' prayer is fulfilled, and the Kingdom of Heaven comes to earth as it is in Heaven.**

When Jesus Christ becomes your success and your treasure, goodness and mercy will follow you all the days of your life. When Jesus becomes your success, there will be no chance of failure. I count a day successful, not by how many people I reach. I count a day successful, not by new programs I start. I count a day successful, not by returning all the phone calls at the office or something like that. I count a day successful if I have tithed two and one-half hours to God. If I have given to Him, fellowshipped with Jesus, then Jesus takes care of my success.

When you are in this place, God begins to be your life manager because you are only concerned about your relationship with Him. The degree to which you can crucify your flesh is the degree to which you can really enjoy your life.

Genesis 11:4

They said, "Come, let us build for ourselves a city and a tower whose top will reach into Heaven, and let us make for ourselves a name, otherwise we will be scattered abroad over the face of the whole earth."

Building a city was not their problem. The problem was that they wanted to do it for themselves. This is our problem. Sometimes we want to do God's work, not for God. We want to do God's work not for God's people. We want to do God's work for ourselves – so that we can look good. Sometimes it is a selfish motivation. The problem at the Tower of Babel was that they wanted to do it for themselves. **God can give everything to those who will not make it an idol.**

Whenever I see a successful person, or a prosperous person I always stand in awe. I experience awe, especially if they are a Christian, because I wonder what they had to go through for God to be able to trust them with that. Conversely, I was in an airport and overheard someone whining and complaining about their lack of this and their lack of that. Whenever you fall into the same negativity, you need to get in the face of God, because it is possible that there is something in your heart God needs to reveal. God cannot entrust you with success because you will make it an idol in your life. You will make it an Us thing, Me, or I.

So, God cannot give it to you!

Genesis 11:6-7

The Lord said, "Behold, they are one people, and they all have the same language. And this is what they began to do, and now nothing which they purpose to do will be impossible for them. Come, let Us go down and there confuse their language, so that they will not understand one another's speech."

Notice the Scripture says, "Let Us go down and confuse them." For years I did not see this, but now I understand. He is saying your "us" is a small "us," comparatively speaking. Because God is the Trinity. God is saying, "Let Us show what a big Us can do."

Unity is a spiritual principle. If the people unify, God is saying nothing will be impossible for them and when the people unify, nothing will stop them. Note again the Scripture, "The Lord said behold they are one people and they all have the same language and this is what they began to do. Now nothing which they have purposed to do is impossible for them."

God is saying that We (Father, Son, Holy Spirit) have to stop them because if they unify nothing will be impossible for them!

God, in a sense, could not stop them, so He had to confuse them. He did this so that they would not unify, because if they unified, nothing would be impossible for them. So, God came down and confused their language.

Because nothing would be impossible for these SELFish people, He had to stop the unity. A question that the Tower of Babel people should have asked themselves, and a great self-examination question to ask oneself is, "With you finding your place and purpose in life and your calling, what is the goal of your success? If you say, "Lord I am called to do this or that," ask yourself, "What is my purpose in doing that? What is the goal for my success?" If you do not have a goal for your success, your success will master you. If you do not give a goal to your purpose, if you do not give a goal to your promised land, and if you do not give a goal to your fruitfulness, you will never find true success. You will never find life-changing influence in the world around you. Do not just pray, "Lord, make me rich so I can have nice things." But rather pray, "Lord, make me rich so I can help alleviate world hunger. Lord, make me rich so I can fund more projects for your Kingdom. Lord, give me that particular job so I can influence that area of life. Lord, make me a famous musician, not just because I like to play music, but so I can flood the earth with Godly music. Lord, make me a famous musician so I can invade the music industry with Jesus."

If you do not have a goal for your success, it will become your master. Jesus gave you His life; therefore, you have no right to live! You were cursed to hell. You were damned to hell because of your sin. Jesus, in exchange for your life, gave you His. Therefore, you have no right to live except Him through you.

It is also a lifestyle that is antithetical to the world systems around us. This means that, when you start living the life Jesus has called you to, you will often look stupid. It looks backwards to those who are living a life consumed with Us. It looks difficult to those who do not know the discipline of the Lord.

161

Your success is to be a platform for you to reveal Jesus and His Kingdom in a greater way. What is the goal of your fruitfulness? God will not entrust to you what you cannot lay down for Him. If you want to proceed to advance in a certain area of life, show God that He is Lord over that area. Then He can and will prosper you. I have gotten into some things before and I said, "Lord, I just want to stop for a second. This is Yours, this is Yours, it is not mine." Why do you think He needs to get a tithe from us all the time? Because no man can serve two masters. The Scripture says that you cannot serve God and mammon [money] (Mathew 6:24).

In all our doing and in all our accomplishments, what is the goal? Why should God entrust success to you? Is your heart ready for that? If you are saying, "God, I need a breakthrough in a certain area of my life, I am just not financially getting it. I cannot find a job." Whether it is money or any other area of life where you need a breakthrough, search your heart and say, "Lord, is there anything that I possess that I need to handover to You? Is there anything in me that I need to surrender over to You?" You spend that carpet time, that closet time with God, and you let Him deal with your heart. There are seasons in my life where I have to do it daily – literally daily. "Oh God, I got proud again. Oh Lord, I am taking some the glory for myself."

It is very subtle, but when you turn everything over to the Lord and you seek first His Kingdom, you will see incredible things happen through you, because God wants to reach the world, but He needs yielded vessels. He needs people who will say, "I will not touch Your glory. My goal is to make you famous, Jesus." That is what He needs!

When we get to that broken place before God and we live in a state of brokenness, then His Kingdom can come on earth as it is in Heaven.

162

I am not saying this is easy. Everything about our existence seems to force us into seeing the world only through our own eyes. We cannot live outside our body. We cannot view life through the eyes of another. We cannot stop our own thoughts from flowing through our head. It seems that God is asking the impossible.

Of course He is asking the impossible. God is, after all, the God of the impossible! He calls those things that are not, as though they were! He separates the water in the Red Sea so that an entire nation can walk through on dry land (Exodus 14:21). He causes the sun to stand still in the sky so that Joshua can have the daylight he needs to win the battle (Joshua 10:13). With the sound of a trumpet, He brings down the strongest walls in the ancient world at Jericho (Joshua 6:20). God is the God of the impossible!

Activation Points:

1. List five ways that you "get in God's way" when He is working in your life. For example, maybe it is unbelief that stops God's power from flowing through you.

2. Find a Scripture verse that helps you learn how to overcome your own self-destruction.

3. List five things in your life that you believe God wants to do for you that are absolutely impossible in your own strength.

4. Find a Scripture verse that declares the ability of God to achieve the impossible for each of the five.

CHAPTER FOURTEEN:

THE TREE SYSTEM

God is a result-oriented God. He is not just a theoretical God. He is definitely not a religious God. He is absolutely practical. He wants results. He wants to see people saved. He wants the Kingdom to come. He wants us to prosper.

History Makers Academy is a ministry that rewires people for supernatural living that achieves real results. We actually train and equip the body of Christ. We are equipping the body of Christ, not just to sit in church, as good as that is and as much as we need that, but we are training and equipping you to discover your calling, which is your purpose. Then, we train you to be excellent at your purpose.

Excellence is something that has been missing from much of the church for a long time. We need to get back to the place where we are the best at what we do. We should be the best musicians. We should be the best real estate agents. We should run the best rehab centers. We should be the best government leaders. We should be the best educators. Simply put, we should be the best at everything we do.

We should not settle for just enough to get by. We should not let others take our place because we do not want to step up and fight the fight to be excellent. We should be the best educated, the best spoken, the most well written. In short, we should be a true example of God, who created everything and set everything in motion. **We should be the greatest example of Heaven on earth with everything we do.**

Our emphasis is about ministry that goes on beyond the four walls. We place high emphasis on bringing the ministry, that would be in the church, outside to society, redeeming every level of society, redeeming people, and inviting His Kingdom to come. This means that we are the Kingdom carriers. We are those who are going out and doing something.

We can no longer wait for others to step up. We cannot sit and wait for God to raise up someone. The someone He wants to raise up, is you and it is me. We are called to be God's catalyst for change in the world around us.

We can also no longer think that some aspects of culture are too secular or evil for us to have influence. Unless you are talking about the satanic church there is nothing we should exclude ourselves from. For too long we have refused to bring our Christianity into science. As a result, we have a world full of scientist who are denying God and we blame science. We are to blame. These are the areas we need to take back into our worldview. We will not do that through religious arguments, we will do it when we embrace science, like many great Christian thinking scientists did in the past, and formulate arguments that are founded on science.

History Makers Academy has hundreds (possibly thousands – we're not keeping count) of graduates around the world. Much of our ministry is helping people discover what they are called to do. Or at least they have discovered what they feel they need to do, solving a problem in society. Our graduates create ministries, projects, programs, or movements, and all kinds of things that bring Kingdom influence. I have talked about teaching the academy principles. It is not about how many people we can get in the building, but about how much Kingdom we can get beyond the four walls of the church.

We will continue to lose our influence in the world if we continue to hide inside the four walls of the church. While what goes on inside the church building is important – in fact, it is not too much to say and not too critical to say – we are losing our influence because we are not engaging the culture. We must have Christians who are not afraid to engage the culture. We must have Christians who are not afraid of stepping into traditionally secular spheres of influence, and bringing Christian influence back into the marketplace.

This is one of the reasons that I teach **"Why Small is the New Big."** God takes great pleasure in using small churches that can shift on a dime. We need churches that do not have to please the masses. All over the world I am seeing small churches doing big things. It is not that big churches cannot do something, but as my Dad always taught me, it is more difficult with a much greater process to turn a large cruise liner on the water, than a speed boat that you can steer quickly.

Through our academy, we are creating graduates who automatically become part of the History Makers Society. It is not a church. We are the church, but it is like the church without walls, the called out ones, the *"ecclesia."* All of our society members attend local congregations. They have pastors. We major on this. They also have their own ministries and influences in society. We help teach them how to start movements and projects. Many of our society members are creating what we call transformational councils, which are small groups of people, no more than twelve or thirteen people, in cities, in countries, in churches, or outside of churches in homes, that meet once a week for the sole purpose of strategizing Kingdom-building.

We are called to be salt and light. We are supposed to be a value to the community and the world.

A church that is not salt and light to the world is not the church. A church, that is not meeting the needs of the community and the needy in the community, is not performing the duties of the church. We have to get back to the place of changing those around us with the power of the Gospel of the Kingdom. This is the Gospel that sets the captives free, it heals the sick, feeds the hungry, and visits those in prison.

For too long the church has turned a blind eye. During all of that time we have witnessed the church in the West losing more and more of its influence. We have gotten to the point that we now find many Christians who do not know what the basic tenants of the faith are. We have to return to a vibrant church that is capable of changing the world around us. This type of miracle working will revolutionize the culture around us and make the church relevant.

What is the practical process? What do we teach? This teaching is a snippet from our sessions. I teach it to all of our Transformational Councils. It is called the tree system. We major on system building and practical processes. The goal of this particular system is to help any individual create a ministry, program, or organization to help influence society. Some programs and projects are larger, while some are smaller. ALL have influence beyond what we see immediately. ALL matter to God.

The process of starting anything significant begins with the ability to have an organized thought. An organized thought is a mental picture of A to Z and the steps to get there in between. It is not just a dream. It is not just a vision. It is not just a prophecy or a prayer, but it is the ability to see all the steps we need to get through from seed to tree for example.

It is not just seeing the picture. It is doing what it takes to make the vision or the dream come true. It is one thing to be a person who sees the big picture. It is another to be the person who makes the big picture come true. Those are the people for whom God is looking in these latter days.

We teach people to have an encounter with God. That is really the biggest and most important thing, because you do not want to do anything that God has not told you to do. You do not want to do anything in vain. So, we encourage having a personal encounter with God. Out of that encounter should come some type of vision or commission. Like Isaiah who had an encounter with God. The Lord said, "Who will go for us?" Isaiah said he would go (Isaiah 6:8). Then, God sent him on the mission. The same thing happened with Ezekiel. He has an encounter with God. God says, "I am sending you to these people. Here is what you are to do." (Ezekiel 2:4). We believe the same thing.

Let's consider an individual's program and influence like a great big tree. The tree is where we actually begin.

Luke 13:18-19

So He was saying, "What is the kingdom of God like, and to what shall I compare it? It is like a mustard seed, which a man took and threw into his own garden; and it grew and became a tree, and THE BIRDS OF THE AIR NESTED IN ITS BRANCHES."

I love that. Jesus is trying to determine how He can best explain the Kingdom of God.

The birds nesting in the branches are a great example of the branches reaching out into the community, or into the city, or into the nation, and giving shelter and rest to the society. Another interesting understanding of the "birds of the air" is that they could also represent the demonic powers. When something is Kingdom you attract both good people and demonic things. You attract the birds of prey! You attract the birds of the air. I have never met a single minister or anointed movement that does not have great branches and big birds showing up, squawking, and making noise around the ministry. There are always vultures and scavengers.

The Tree

What is the tree? The tree is the macro-finished product – the big picture. This is the finished ministry which can be as big as your dreams and faith will allow. What it is going to look like, the influence it will have, who it will be reaching, all of these details go into determining what the tree will look like – exactly what God has shown you.

We know that when there is Kingdom DNA and it is really the Kingdom of God, as far as the tree is concerned, the tree did not just show up fully developed and fully grown. The tree began somewhere. That significant tree actually began as an insignificant seed. Even Jesus Christ, when He came, came as a baby. When God wants to do something big, He always starts small. When God wants to grow something from small to big, He grows it incrementally. So if the tree is stage two, stage one is the seed – the tiny, little, insignificant seed that you can barely see, which came first.

The seed that Jesus was talking about is actually the smallest of all the other garden plants. Another Scripture reference for this seed is found in John.

John 12:24

"Truly, truly, I say to you, unless a grain of wheat falls into the earth and dies, it remains alone; but if it dies, it bears much fruit."

Isn't that interesting? **In the Kingdom of God, you have to die to produce.** To get resurrection life, you have to go to the cross. To get significance, you have to start small. This is why the seed is so crucial, the seed processes the beginning stage of your ministry, project, or movement. It is how the process of your calling begins. The tree, this great ministry, begins as a tiny seed. When we talk about "unless a seed falls into the ground and dies it cannot bear much fruit," we are talking about the process of death, not literal death, but laying down your life in exchange for people. We are talking about laying down your life either through prayer and intercession or sacrifice. Remember what Isaiah 43:3-4 says, "Because you are such a precious seed, in exchange for your death I will give Cush and Seba, nations, in exchange for your life." This is all the seed process.

The Seed

The seed process is the dying to self, and even the dying to ministry. Imagine, you are trying to start a ministry and the first step is to die to ministry. The first step is death! You say, "God, you showed me a vision and now You want me to lay it down?" Remember Abraham and Isaac – it is the particular process for procuring your purpose (Genesis 22:2).

Sacrifice means giving up something of value of yours for the benefit of others. It can be money. It can be time. It can be giving up your will and your way so that God can show you a new way to do ministry or a project.

It sounds easy, here on the written page, but it is not. It truly takes great character to sacrifice for the good of others. When you are taking on people who have addiction issues or even just sin issues, there will be times of extreme trial. People spend years destroying their lives and they are not restored overnight. It often takes as long to overcome a sin or addiction, as it took to get bound up by the same. This means that you will have to show great patience, great love, and great grace to help people be restored truly to the life God has for them. It is not simply a matter of prayer. It is a matter of great work.

The other way we die is through prayer and intercession for the people we are trying to reach through that ministry. We have no right to minister to a people for whom we have not first prayed, or in a metaphorical manner, for whom we have not died. You can have a budget, a plan, funding, a building, all the right stuff, but real ministry is rooted in the spirit realm. This is where the real work is being done.

You have no right even to open your mouth, until you sit where they sit and until you eat what they eat. It is amazing, Ezekiel gets this incredible commission to minister to Israel and what does he do? He goes and sits in their presence where they sit for one week and says nothing! This prophet goes into ministry and says nothing for an entire seven days (Ezekiel 3:15-16). It is part of the seed process and the other is the hiddenness. The hiddenness is critical in the death (and consequent life) of the seed.

When I was a child in school, they gave us all a seed. I was so excited. We had a little foam cup and we wrote our name on the cup. We got some soil, filled the cup with it, and then we buried the seed. I wanted to see the plant, but the process for having the plant, however, was to bury the seed.

When you go to launch a ministry, a project, or whatever, it is going to require a season of hiddenness. There is a lot that goes on behind the scenes before anybody sees it. If you do not honor the process of the "hiddenness and death behind the scenes," you are not going to have a ministry that lasts for a long time. Or it will not go the distance that it could.

What happens is the seed gets buried in the process of hiddenness. At the seed stage, the work you are doing on your project is hidden. You are researching the people group you are trying to reach. You might be going to school to learn more about the processes or to get a degree to qualify you to work in your chosen area. Maybe you are praying and doing the intercession needed to plant a ministry or a project. It is all the hidden work; you are not telling a lot of people about the work yet. You are asking God for clarity and you are dealing with your insecurities. You are mapping it out. These are all the things that take place in the prayer closet.

The Bible says, "Go and pray to your Father." And where is He? It says to pray to Him in secret. This is the seed place, where you secretly weep for the nation you are trying to reach. You weep for the family you are praying for. You suffer and sacrifice for your calling.

The Roots

Step two should be pretty obvious. The root system is very interesting. In my school project, I had a foam cup. Each day I felt a bit of a failure, because each day I was watering it and putting it in the sun, and nothing was growing. Days went by and nothing showed to be growing. As a child, I finally cracked that foam cup open to get the seed out. Only then did I find that there was a lot going on behind the scenes! The seed had been busy developing a very complex root system! Through this life lesson, you can see that the seed must be hard at work, building up a foundation that will extend to the actual project, ministry, and purpose.

When you look at a construction site, if you have ever had construction going on outside your house, the bulk of the time they spend establishing a tall building is spent underground. The workers are down there, where you cannot see them, for days and days and days. You begin to wonder if the building is ever going to be built. It begins with the foundation.

You will find the root system in Jeremiah 17.

Jeremiah 17:7-8

Blessed is the man who trusts in the Lord and whose trust is in the Lord, for he shall be like a tree planted by the water, that extends its roots by a stream.

173

The root system is the foundational, preparatory work that goes on behind the scenes. The ministry or project is not necessarily public yet. It is not a fully functioning project. It consists of the developing of identity. This is hugely important! Growing roots is the process of asking and answering many questions. Who are you as a ministry? Who is on your team? You are having some team meetings, maybe. You are meeting with your pastor or your leader, and you are discussing what is the identity of this ministry? Who are you?

The company Nike really majored on who they are, their identity. If you do a tour of the Nike headquarters the people do not actually talk about themselves there. They talk about Nike. They talk about the history of Nike. They talk about what they are presently doing and their future goals. I have heard that even the custodian can tell you all about Nike. They know who they are.

Foundational work is extremely important. Just like when you build a building, if the foundation is not built right, the building will not function properly. If you do not know who you are, you will lose track of who you are to be, who God has called you to be, when you begin to go and do something. Develop an identity, which can involve research, creating a mission statement, and creating a vision statement. Usually the mission statement is one line. The vision statement is usually shorter. Check out Nike's: "Just Do It."

Then you have to do your research. Those will be times where you are having to steal time and do the hard work of real research. The kids are in bed, nobody is around, and the roots are stretching out. At this stage, you are probably also trying to network with key people who can help you advance your program. Maybe God is bringing people across your path who will be part of your leadership team. The gathering of a team is happening during this phase as well.

There is something else that goes on behind the scenes in the root system, which is character development. This is where God will test you to see if you have the character to handle the plant and the success that comes from the project. This is where the testing goes on and you cannot quite explain to people around you just what you are going through. You know you are being developed because of the greatness of what God has called you.

Shortcutting this portion of developing the roots can be fatal. Many previous organizations got a great idea and immediately started the project. They did not go through the character building stage and, as a result, the ministry or the project or the movement never became what they could have been, because the character of the leadership was not properly developed.

The Shoot

Stage three is the shoot stage. As a child, I planted another seed in that foam cup, and this time gave it the time to go through the process. Eventually that seed and its root system became a tiny shoot that pushed through the soil and could be seen.

This is the stage where your project starts to "remember" and becomes visible. It is not yet considered successful, as there is no fruit on it, but you are getting somewhere. A little ministry has begun. You are watering and you have it in sunlight, but it is God who is giving it growth.

The shoot, this is the point of the project where you have established the beginnings of your ministry. It is not where you want it to be, but you have begun. God is controlling the growth. He is giving the increase. You have passed some character tests. To the degree that your roots and foundation are properly in alignment, is the degree and speed the shoot will be growing.

Character and private life will determine the public result. This is where you are doing a little bit of marketing and promotion. You are learning how to promote and you are learning how to market what you are doing. You are not keeping it a secret.

The project is public at this point, but it is not really recognized. Maybe the people in your church know about it because it was printed in your bulletin one Sunday. Maybe the pastor mentioned it from the pulpit. The shoot stage is when the project or ministry really needs consistent care and attention. It needs to be cultivated. It needs to be kept healthy. Even secular society understands, that when you are starting a business, you are there day and night. You are practically sleeping under the desk. You are putting all you have into that shoot because you are beginning to gain momentum. It needs consistent care and attention.

Part of this process involves pulling the weeds that naturally develop. There is no way to avoid the weeds. They are part of the world we live in. Remember, it is easy to get distracted taking care of little things that have no part of the bigger picture. It takes discernment to know how to do what only you can do. As you develop your team it is important to remember that every team member has his or her place.

True leaders have to learn how to delegate projects and work to team members. If the leader insists on being involved heavily in every step of the process the process begins to bog down. You actually become a bottle neck that keeps much of the critical work from happening. A team has to work as a team. A leader has to inspire members of the team to do some of the work, especially those parts of the work that are not glamorous. Everyone wants to do what is seen as important. A leader has to inspire the team to do the little things that do not seem important. Otherwise, the foundation will not be properly laid. If the foundation is not properly laid you will be forced to go back and fix issues that never should have arisen. Reworking the foundation after the building is built is expensive, time consuming, and exhausting to everyone involved. This is one of the problems that often cause ministries, projects, and movements to fall apart.

This is also where the enemy will come in, try to intimidate, and destroy the ministry. He will try to fight you and get you to quit. If, however, you have a strong foundation and a strong root system, you will not quit despite the wind and the waves. This is where you should be developing a web site, even if it is just one page, that says you exist. Web sites are today's business card. If you do not have a web site, consider yourself nonexistent. God may know you. Your name might be written in the Book of Life, but you will not be recognized here on this earth.

Business cards are important. I was against business cards for a long time, but now I have one. It is a lot quicker and more professional, than finding a pen and writing down your phone number and your email address. They should share who you are, your web site, and your contact details. This is the world that we live in.

At this stage, you are looking for money. You are either looking for financial sponsorship, or you are registering as a charity. You might do grant research to see if your project is something the government will give you money to do. You may be surprised that you can get grant funding. It is challenging because there is a lot involved. You have to learn how to apply or bring on an expert to do the research and complete the application. We had to do that with our first Transformation Council. You must look into that.

This is a fragile time – so there is a great need for continued prayer and support. One of the most important things you can do during the shoot process is be consistent. Plants need consistent sunlight and consistent watering. The most important thing you can do is be consistent.

The Plant

Stage four is the plant stage. The shoot is maturing. This is where the program is visible, it is maturing. People are starting to take notice of it. People are aware of it in the church, in the city, maybe even in the nation. It requires less controlling, hands-on protection. It is a fully functioning social enterprise. It is serving the church, but it is beginning to branch out into the community. Things are not fully fruitful yet, but it is its own self-governing organization.

You still attend the local church, you have a pastor, but you are the pastor of your project. It is out there. It has a name. Maybe you have some grant funding, some government funding, and sponsorship. You have a fully functioning team. You are recognized in the community because you held an event – maybe like a kick-off.

I challenge our people to hold a kick-off event on a citywide level. One of our History Makers in Toronto, Aisha Francis, did this. She invited the city councilmen, the mayor, key people, representatives from the local university, and she presented her project called "Project Restore FIBI" which is a program that helps rehabilitate families that are impacted by incarceration. These secular leaders came to the event. Christian leaders came out. Aisha had a great time giving a presentation. Her program is now formally recognized because of this initial event. You would be surprised at the networking that goes on in meetings like this and the doors that are opened.

It is important that you do not get discouraged at this point in the process. Fundraising is often the hardest part. Remember, people are not as excited about your work as you are. Often people have trouble getting the vision. Many people fall aside during this stage. They talk to a few people about money, they are met with no response, and they give up.

Any person who is involved in sales will tell you that getting to yes is very discouraging. It often takes hundreds of No's to get to a Yes. If you do not have great character, and thick skin, here is where you start to not believe in the work God has given you. There is no magic moment during this process. It is very much a numbers game. If you talk to enough people, if you inspire enough people, if you find the right group of people to talk to, then you will find the funding.

It is also important for you to try different approaches to fundraising. If one pitch does not work, try another pitch. Just because you like a certain approach to your ministry or project, does not mean that other people will. Be adaptable. Be able to shift directions in fundraising at the drop of a hat.

The Tree

Another thing we do with our Transformation Council is we get them to become visible because now we are shifting from the plant stage to stage five, the tree stage. We have the whole council purchase a gift for the city leader, the mayor. We bring the gift and present it to him or her to honor them. Honor is powerful when entering a city to serve. Even God will fight against you if you are dishonoring the city leaders, Christian or not Christian.

Honor is actually the protocol for entering the city. What we do is go and meet with the mayor, we sit down with him/her. (S)he is usually shocked that there are people offering free labor and programs to reach out to the community. That blows him/her away. Then we present our gift and say, "Is there anything we can pray with you for?" We pray for him/her right on the spot, or we promise to pray later. We have been accepted and been given his/her permission or blessing. When that happens and there is the proper authority given, guess what is next? God begins to bless your work because of His spiritual law and principle. You might just get an email or a phone call with an invitation from the mayor to come to key events and meetings and be a presence there.

This is what it is to reach out to a community – to show up. This is the part that is difficult. You have to be a strong, thick tree to handle the world outside of the church. I will be honest with you; it is way more comfortable inside the church.

Inside the church is a culture you understand. It is where you think alike. It is where you understand the end goal of leading people into the Kingdom of God. Your work, however, is purposefully designed to go beyond the four walls of the church. That means you need to learn to speak to another culture. You need to learn what motivates them to get engaged. You need to learn what their needs are. You have to learn how to minister to them in a manner they can accept.

As big and awesome as it is, the tree is a servant, existing to bear fruit that serves the community. At this stage, you still have naysayers, but you also get people coming to find rest and to find shade in this ministry, or project, or organization that you have produced.

Do not despise small beginnings. **We are all given different capacities, different abilities, five talents, ten talents, whatever it is.** It is like a lady in Bulgaria, with whom we work, who did not have what she thought was a significantly large-enough idea. All she did was take what she had in her hands. She had a pen. She had some paper. She began to write out her understanding of the Kingdom of God and the Gospel of Salvation. She created this beautiful pamphlet. Since the Bible says that the Gospel of the Kingdom will be preached to the whole world, she decided to hand out these pamphlets and letters. She said, "This is what I can do." So she did it. She is a part of one of our Transformational Councils in Bulgaria. She began to hand them out. Before long she created a system to do her calling, and that seed became a tree in the form of sixty thousand of her pamphlets having been handed out. Some people who received the pamphlets and read them, died not too long after receiving them, but they heard the Gospel message presented, often for the first time. She now has a goal for the branches of that tree to reach out and cover the nation of Bulgaria, city by city. Every city we are going into and opening up, she is there. She is going to use her system there, using these pamphlets to reach out. This is her contribution. It has become a tree.

There are some projects that are smaller. One of our Transformational Council members in Bulgaria started offering free legal services. They picked up a phone, contacted some Christian lawyers, and asked them to give one day a week, working out of the office of a local church, and offering free legal counsel to single parents. The lawyers agreed and they give their time on Tuesday. The Transformational Council members opened up child care on Tuesdays so that the parents could get legal counsel, with the children being looked after at the same time.

I know a custodian in a high school who became a great tree. All he did was talk to the students –simply that. He smiled at students. He became a listening ear for those students. He eventually became a mentor to some of them. You cannot tell me that when he gets to Heaven that God is not going to honor the seed in his life that became a great tree.

The Kingdom of God is a tangible substance, a tangible force that is designed to take over and turn the world upside down.

Welcome to how to build the Kingdom of God.

Activation Points:

(There are no individual Activation Points associated with this chapter. The Ministry Team will work with you directly to develop your own Tree.)

SECTION FOUR:

UNDERSTANDING SOCIETAL AND NATIONAL TRANSFORMATION

CHAPTER FIFTEEN:
REDEEMING THE LAND

God not only wants us to redeem the land, God expects us to redeem the land! Jesus has paid the price so that we can redeem the land. To do anything less is to live a life of compromise with our calling. It is to live a life that does not meet the measures that God has called us to.

For too long we have thought that our calling was only to pray. Do not get me wrong! God expects us to pray. He commands us to pray. What I am talking about is the fact that once we have prayed, we are not finished. Prayer is the beginning point. Once we have prayed, we must act. We must follow through, we must become the prayer we have prayed, and change the area of the world where we have influence. We must follow our prayers with boldness and action. We must be Jesus in our sphere of influence.

All religions pray, so why is it different when Christians pray? When we pray, we are partnering with a real God. God's prayer agent is the Holy Spirit. We need the help of the Holy Spirit. The challenge is sometimes we pray in ignorance, because we do not understand the tools that are needed in the moment to be strategically successful.

Sometimes we pray about things that God has already done. Sometimes we pray about things He has already told us to do. Sometimes we are begging God to come down and do something that He has instead told us to do.

I used to think that if I raised my voice enough, if I suffered enough in prayer, then somehow I could get God to do something. I could twist His arm as if revival were His problem. Now I believe in raising your voice and praying fervently. I believe in knocking on the King's door. I do pray that way, but that is only out of passion and humbling my flesh.

It is actually possible that when we limit prayer to just shouting and fervency, sometimes we can begin to border on pagan prayers, because this is how the pagans pray. If they can pressure and abase themselves enough, like the Prophets of Baal, they think they will be answered. You see, sometimes a moment of faith can do what many hours of prayer cannot do. A strategic prayer of faith can do what it sometimes takes people years to do in prayer.

You see, because God is real, and because our relationship with Him is real, it does not require us to convince God to act on our behalf. Part of being in relationship with God is the concept that we are doing His will, to the best of our ability, on a daily basis. When we are doing God's will, we do not have to convince Him to move on our behalf. He has already set things in motion to move on our behalf. Prayer that seeks to convince God is not faith-filled prayer. **Faith-filled prayer is prayer that understands the nature and will of God.** It is prayer that builds faith in others, but in us, it is merely a conversation with God of belief in Him.

Let's look at an example. Suppose you are at church and you have a car to drive to and from church. Let's say the goal is to move your car from where we are, down the street to a nice restaurant. You say the car weighs a certain tonnage, and it is a very heavy thing to move. So, you recruit ten of the strongest men you know to help you pick up the car to move it. You go out and sit in the seat with your hands on the steering wheel, and the strong men begin to lift the car. On the sidewalk, a large group of people is praying for the car to be moved successfully. Then one of your friends come out to the car. Your friend is very wise, and he asks, "Hey, what are you doing? I appreciate that you want to move the car. If you do it this way, you might eventually move the car. But let me help you make the job easier." Then your friend pulls out a car key, and puts it into the ignition. It's such a tiny key, but it is the right key. He turns over the ignition and the motor starts running. You no longer need ten strong people. Your friend moves the car and you are impressed.

This is how you need to see prayer. **Sometimes, to do something big, you do not need as much yelling and pushing.** You just need the right key. You just need understanding of what is the right tool at the right moment.

This is the beauty of having a relationship with God. When you truly love God and truly have a relationship with Him, you know that you cannot manipulate Him into working on your behalf. You know that He wants what is best for you. You know that He wants to reveal Himself to mankind. You know that He has designed the Universe to speak His name and to tell of His wonders.

When you live in that understanding, you merely need to connect with God. Think of a marriage. If you and your spouse are in a right relationship, you do not have to yell at each other to get done what needs to be done. Often what needs to be done gets done without any discussion at all. That is what is beautiful about being in a relationship – it does not require great effort or manipulation to get what needs to be done. I am not saying that there is not a lot of work involved in keeping in a right relationship with God.

Biblically, we understand that there are different kinds of prayer. One of the greatest foundational keys, when understanding prayer, is the word authority. You must couple authority with faith so that you understand your legal rights. When you pray, especially for something large, you first remind yourself of your legal authority. Even God functions by legalities. That is why He came as a man – it had to be done legally as a man to take back, what man lost – the keys of the Kingdom. This is the only way spiritually that the keys (that is, authority) could be returned to us.

You have authority. Prior to the cross is what I call the pre-cross commission. The pre-cross commission was to heal the sick, cast out demons, and cleanse lepers. It was restricted to the house of Israel (Matthew 10:5-8). Now it is after the cross, after Jesus died and rose again – post-cross commission. It is now not only open season for miracles to all nations, but we are also given greater authority.

Matthew 28:18-20

"All authority has been given to Me in Heaven and on earth. Go therefore and make disciples of all the nations, baptizing them in the name of the Father and the Son and the Holy Spirit, teaching them to observe all that I commanded you,"

What are we to do? We are to disciple all nations. Every sphere of life, everywhere we go, we are to be "Teaching them to observe…" Let me give you an example of this. If I were to come to your house, I have to take my shoes off to enter your house. In my culture, however, we keep our shoes on. When I come to your house I can take them off, even though I believe I can keep them on. Why am I taking them off at your house? I take them off because I am coming on your property where you have authority. Therefore, I must observe your custom.

When the Bible says, in the Great Commission, "Teaching them to observe," Matthew 28:20, it means teaching other people to observe our values, to observe Heavenly principles, and to observe Biblical principles. So, when I come to your house, I must observe your values as long as I am under your authority. This is why it is so profound that Jesus says to teach the whole world to observe Biblical values and principles! The whole world is now under His authority and jurisdiction.

What gives me the right to enforce Heaven's values everywhere I go? I have this authority because the whole earth is under the authority of Jesus. Therefore, we have a legal right to teach the principles of the Kingdom of God everywhere. We are not to restrict the Kingdom of God to just our churches and our prayer meetings. To restrict the Kingdom of God merely to our churches and prayer meetings – that is simply religion.

Jesus was really clear in the limitation He gave to us. Go into all the world and teach them to observe. **We are commanded to teach the world.** We have a work to do. We have only the limitation of this world. God did not call you and me to save the moon. We are to change this world.

Jesus' dream is for the glory and the knowledge of God to cover the earth as the waters cover the sea. How are we going to accomplish this? We, as carriers of that Kingdom, must go out! Bringing the Kingdom of God with us is our responsibility.

Now, if we are going to venture out there, if we are going out as sheep among wolves, we better know how to pray. We must believe in our prayers. We must believe in the God of our prayers. And, we must use strategy!

This is the part that most Christians miss. We have been taught that our job is to pray for God to move. I am not saying that we should not pray. We should definitely be praying! In fact, we should be praying more and harder than ever before. We should be waging war in the Heavenlies through prayer. This is critical for the survival of the church and for the advent of revival.

Just as much as we need to pray, we need to be about the Father's business. Jesus spent hours in prayer. He withdrew regularly from the crowds and His disciples to spend time in fellowship and prayer with God. Yet, when He was finished with His time in prayer, He came back to the people and He BROUGHT the

Kingdom of God to them. He did the works of the Kingdom every minute of every day. He did not sit around and say, "God, I asked You to do this. What is the problem?" He did not just talk to God about the solutions, He became the solution for us all.

This is what we are talking about here – marriage between prayer and action. **We need an understanding that intercession is talking to God, seeking His face and direction, and then doing the work of the Kingdom.** One without the other will never be as effective as both of them together in proper alignment. Covering ourselves in prayer and then reaching out to the lost around us and changing the world as we know it is the marriage of prayer with action.

There is a difference in talking about fighting a war and actually fighting a war. It is easy to talk about how we should do something, while it is another thing to actually do it. If we are bringing everyone to the church to be saved and changed and our outreach ends there, it is less dependent on strategy than if we are taking the church into the community – into our sphere of influence.

If we are just bringing people to the church and not taking the church to people, the approach is completely different. If we are going into the world as light and life, then we need to be prayed up and we need to have strategy. It is great to simply believe that God will protect us. It is, however, true that we need to approach the lost, outside the walls of the church, in a strategic manner that gives them the opportunity to see God move in their lives and in the community where we are.

You have authority to disciple your nation. The definition for authority is your right to rule. It is your right to have a successful business. It is your right to open up a community to the Kingdom of God. You have the right to rule! This is very important.

You need more than just the right, however. You also need the power! A police officer has two things: a badge and a gun. The badge represents his authority. All he has to do is flash that badge and he has the right to rule. When people see the badge they understand his right. Why does he need a gun? If he has authority, why does he need power? He sometimes needs the power to back up and enforce his authority. If somebody wants to oppose his authority, he can use the proper power up to and including his gun.

In the same way, we have authority. We have a badge in the spirit realm. It is the name of Jesus! We have the authority. We have the right, but sometimes we are opposed. When we go out to transform a community, when we go out to do more than just pray inside our building, we have authority. But when we are opposed, we need power. Prayer and strategy is power! Prayer and strategy backs up your authority.

God has called each of us to a sphere of influence. God has anointed us to do what He has called us to do. At the same time, He expects us to be experts in the area of our calling. If you are called to be a surgeon it is not enough to merely pray before surgery. You have to study the art of medicine. You have to study how surgery is performed. You have to practice under the authority of someone who actually knows how to and has performed surgery in the past. Then, and only then, are you allowed to perform surgery.

The same holds true in every sphere of influence. The time and requirements are different from sphere to sphere, but you still need to be knowledgeable and skilled. You still need to have more than prayer to uphold you. If you are a lawyer, you cannot tell the judge that God has told you that your client is innocent. Rather, you have to prove, using the tools of a lawyer, the facts, the evidence, and the law, to prove to the judge that your client is innocent. Expertise is required. We can never forget this. We must be the most prepared people in the room when we come before a city council to talk about an issue where we are wanting to bring change.

In the Kingdom of God, strategy is so important. Strategy in both prayer and our actions. There is something powerful that happens when the church operates in "organized action."

Proverbs 13:23

Abundant food is in the fallow ground of the poor, but it is swept away by injustice. He who withholds his rod hates his son, But he who loves him disciplines him diligently.

What an amazing Scripture!

Much food is in the ground of the poor. This means that prosperity, success, and victory are available to anyone. It is not limited to a certain class or demographic of people. A person can have success anywhere. Why do some people not prosper since much prosperity is available to all? The Bible says it is swept away by injustice! Therefore, we understand that we can prosper and have results whether we are in South America, Latin America, Central America, America, Canada, Bulgaria – anywhere in the world. That success is available anywhere. Why do we not see it? We do not see it because it is possible that it is being swept away by injustice.

In this context, injustice could be replaced with the word "disorganization." That is to say that any injustice on earth is seen by God as disorganization compared to God's original design for mankind.

This means that even though we have opportunity all around us. Sometimes what we know matters, and a lack of organization affects our results. Sometimes what we do not know matters. Sometimes our problem is how we wrongly organize or disorganize. God sees injustice as disorganization. God sees disorganization as injustice. The redemption of the land, how you open up a community to the Kingdom of God, begins and ends with organized intercession and organized action.

Again, as an example, think of a city government. If the government offices are disorganized, they cannot perform the functions for which they were created. If they do not perform the functions for which they were created, then injustice follows. If the city water department does not function properly, it means that ultimately water is not where it is needed. This is injustice, because the people of the city do not have access to clean water, and clean water is critical to life.

There are two types of intercession, and we can do both: prayer and action.

Therefore, intercession is not just prayer. Sometimes intercession is action. For example, Jesus did not just weep and intercede in the garden, He actually physically went to the cross. He both prayed and acted. What is fascinating about the action of Jesus is that it was not violent – it was not using weapons. It was using a weapon that was totally different than what was expected. The Sadducees thought that Jesus was going to conquer through war. They even tried to initiate the war. Then Jesus did the exact opposite.

For example, sometimes when you deal with a spirit of Jezebel, you might be tempted to think that you need to address her personally or "bind" her. When in actuality, sometimes a form of high level warfare is to ignore her, or function in acts of honor and love towards the person she is working through. There are different tools for different situations when it comes to possessing or redeeming the land. Always there is prayer and then there is action. Both can be considered intercession.

Everything in the Kingdom ultimately comes back to doing. That is why the Bible exhorted us to be doers of the Word, not merely hearers. While it is important to hear the Word, to understand the Word of God, it is more important to do the Word of God. It is more important to be the Gospel to the world. It is not enough for them to hear about Jesus, they must see Him. They must see Him in a program that feeds the hungry. They must see Him in a program that brings legal help to the needy. They must see Him in a program that houses the homeless.

That is why Jesus talked about actually reaching out to the hurting of the world, rather than encouraging them to go and be fed. Hearing and talking alone are never enough. We must be doers of the Word. Doing the Word is a form of intercession because it allows people to see Jesus clearly in every situation.

Intercession is not just prayer as we win back the land. It is also action in the face of injustice. Sometimes it can appear very strange and we can feel very persecuted. Abraham was told to go to a foreign land (Genesis 12:1). Isaac went as well. Joseph was sold into slavery. Imaging leaving your homeland and going to a foreign land, and they do not speak your language, and they do not have the same skin color.

Imagine, Joseph being sold into slavery (Genesis 37:28). He goes into a land that is not his own. He suffers the cultural differences. What a tragedy! Their gods are different from his God. Their form of government is different. Everything about the culture of Egypt is different from the culture of Joseph. Yet, Joseph was God's great secret. He endured intercession. Everything Joseph went through in this foreign land was a type of intercession, so that he could be prepared and one day be Prime Minister to redeem and save the land.

Without all of the hardship that Joseph went through, he would not have been prepared for what God had in front of him. Sure, Joseph had seen that his brothers would bow down to him (Genesis 37:5). He had been shown in his dreams that God wanted to do something big in his life. I doubt, however, at the time that Joseph thought God was preparing him to be the second most powerful man in the world. It took years, from the time of the first dream, for God to have Joseph prepared for what He really wanted him to do. It took years in the worst situations to prepare him. It took years of pain and agony that would have broken most of us. One thing we know is that God was always there. We also know, that Joseph never forgot that God was God. We know this because at the end Joseph is the second most powerful man in the world! (Genesis 41:41).

The principle is this: **Everything you go through in this land gives you the authority to put a demand on Heaven for God to give you the land.** You have the right and authority because you are present in the land as living intercession. If you are frustrated in this land, remember you are not here by accident. Take your frustration, take anything you are going through in this land, and use it as an investment. Reap a harvest! Redeem the land!

You are an investment. You are a seed sown so that God can reap a harvest. You are here to form this land. You might ask, "Doesn't it make more sense for God to use me in my own land?" Sometimes God will actually allow you to be thrust from your own land and your own comfort zone, because you have to be a tool of intercession. You are like Daniel interceding in a foreign land. You are like Esther's intercession. That is why God must use you. You must take responsibility for this. Do not just pray, be present in action. Wake up saying, "God wants to use me to redeem the land."

One thing we know is that the land needs to be redeemed. There is no country on the face of the earth that is operating exactly like Heaven. The prayer of Jesus is that God's Kingdom would come on earth as it is in Heaven. Until that is accomplished we have plenty of work to do. It is easy to think that the solution is political. We must remember, however, that politics never raised anybody from the dead! The only solution is for us to bring the

Kingdom into the sphere of influence God has called us to. That is why it is so critical for you to find your sphere and begin to prepare to have influence in that sphere. It is critical that you fulfill the calling of God in your life.

It is not about filling the church with the glory of God. The earth is to be filled with the glory of God.

We know and understand that we wrestle not against flesh and blood (Ephesians 6:12). That is a big statement. We fight against demons – the Bible says we fight against principalities. They are big demons, and they do not go out so easily. They have ruled the land for thousands of years. They do not like it when you come along. They do not like you because you have authority. They know and understand how the spirit realm operates. As long as you remain ignorant, they are happy. They have cursed the land. We can uproot these curses – we must deal with these curses. There is a way to do it. God is wanting to give you tools that others do not have, that they do not even know exist. Because you are a Joseph, God will honor you and your efforts. You are from Joseph's tribe and God is going to raise you up in this land. You are going to solve problems in this economy. In a time of famine, you are going to bring life. In a troubled time, you are going to redeem your family. You, who are from another country, are going to redeem a foreign land.

The same is true for those who are called to their homeland. God is going to use you where you are planted to redeem the land in which you were born. While God called Abraham to another land, He called Moses to the Promised Land, He called David to be the King of Israel – his homeland. Be used where you are, whether it is your homeland or a foreign land.

We know that curses rest on cities and nations. Jesus did not die just to save you. He wants to redeem the land. Let me prove this to you.

Genesis 5:29

Now he called his name Noah, saying, "This one will give us rest from our work and from the toil of our hands arising from the ground which the Lord has cursed."

Can you imagine that God has cursed the earth? All the way back in Genesis, when Adam and Eve first sinned, God said, "Now you are going to have to work by the sweat of your brow." After the curse, it became work by the sweat of your brow. This can be confusing to some because, prior to sin, God told Adam and Eve to work the land. So, what are we talking about here? Prior to sin it was about working their purpose and calling. As a result of the curse, it became about just working for mere survival. Prior to the curse, work was fulfilling destiny and purpose. After the curse, work became slave labor. Working just to get by, even though sometimes we need to work that way to get ahead, that is not your final destination. Your final destination is working in your purpose.

If God has cursed the land, then ultimately only God can redeem the land. We know that God has always chosen to work through His people. He destroyed the world with the flood, but He used Noah to redeem a few chosen people to start fresh. He could have sent an army of angels to rescue Jesus, but He let Him suffer and die.

When we talk about redeeming the land we are talking about setting the land free from the curse or curses that are created by sin. We are talking about liberating the land so that it can reflect the Kingdom of Heaven. What a glorious calling we have – to be used by God to restore the earth to God's original intention for it.

When we discover our work and calling we can begin to win the land and uproot it from curses.

Hosea 4:1-6

Listen to the word of the Lord, O sons of Israel, For the Lord has a case against the inhabitants of the land, Because there is no faithfulness or kindness Or knowledge of God in the land. There is swearing, deception, murder, stealing, and adultery. They employ violence, so that bloodshed follows bloodshed. Therefore the land mourns, And everyone who lives in it languishes Along with the beasts of the field and the birds of the sky, And also the fish of the sea disappear. Yet let no one find fault, and let none offer reproof; For your people are like those who contend with the priest. So you will stumble by day and the prophet also will stumble with you by night; And I will destroy your mother. My people are destroyed for lack of knowledge. Because you have rejected knowledge, I also will reject you from being My priest. Since you have forgotten the law of your God, I also will forget your children.

What an interesting passage. Number one would be said like this: When you are fulfilling your purpose and calling, you are beginning to redeem the land. Number two: Abstaining from sin and living right has great power in the land. Look what it says, "For the Lord has a controversy with the inhabitants of the land. This is my problem with you there is no faithfulness or love." Where there is the absence of love there is a curse.

Where there is the absence of one kingdom, another kingdom rushes in. There is no steadfast love and no knowledge of God in the land. There is swearing, lying, murder, stealing, and committing adultery. Therefore, the land mourns. **This is amazing, our sin affects the land!** When you sin, you are not just impacting your life. You are impacting your workplace, your family life, and even the generations after you. When you sin, something in you and around you dies.

When we sin, we invite curses on the land. This is why we thank God for the blood of Jesus. When the Bible talks about the blood of Jesus still speaking today, it means that our sin can still be forgiven (Hebrews 12:24). The curse that comes as a result of sin can be dealt with. We can pick up our cross. We can approach the throne of mercy and we can be redeemed. The land can be redeemed because of the blood of Jesus. And the curses can be uprooted. Our children's children will suffer in our sin, unless we uproot those curses. That is to say, when you live righteously in an unrighteous land, you begin to redeem the land. This is why we must live right. We are not just living for ourselves. This is why God had a right to destroy Sodom and Gomorrah.

The lesson of Lot is that if there is a critical mass of righteous people, the land can be redeemed (Genesis 18:20-32). Just you being in the land, just you being on the property is part of what is required for the redemption of the land. If you lose your saltiness, if you lose your righteousness, if you behave in sin the way others do, you lose the power to back up your authority. Your prayers do not have power because you have given the enemy the legal right to hinder your prayers.

You will not have authority in the land where there is dishonor, where there is slander, where there is judgment. If you fail to discern the body, who is the body? Your neighbor, the other pastor, all of us are the body. You violate the body then you bring a curse.

Genesis 3:17-18

Then to Adam He said, "Because you have listened to the voice of your wife, and have eaten from the tree about which I commanded you, saying, 'You shall not eat from it'; cursed is the ground because of you; In toil you will eat of it all the days of your life. Both thorns and thistles it shall grow for you; And you will eat the plants of the field;"

This shows the authority we have. Because of our sin, curses are in our lives. God says, "Cursed is the ground because of you. In

199

pain you shall eat of it all day. Thorns and thistles it will bring forth for you." Thorns and thistles are growing because of sin. Let me give you a definition of thorns and thistles. **Thorns and thistles are anything that works against the advancement of the Kingdom.** Some families have thorns and thistles so they are unable to prosper. Or they are unable to marry. Or they are unable to have children. Thorns and thistles are anything that is a result of the curse.

Thorns and thistles can be in cities. You can imagine what the thorns and thistles are growing in Las Vegas – gambling, lust, and all these things. In Canada, thorns and thistles could be the abortion issue, or same sex marriage.

Remember, God wants Heaven to come to earth. That means that God wants us to live in a world that is free from the curse. If He wants that it must mean that it is possible for us to work with Him to create such a world. Jesus would not have prayed for this to be if it were not possible. Never forget that God has called us to create a world that is free from the curses that are on the land. God has called us to live in a world that is ruled the same way as Heaven is ruled.

Thorns and thistles can be uprooted. Even if you are praying for somebody who has not been saved, you may have passed on and gone to Heaven, and they have become old, have grandchildren, and they may be laying on their deathbed. Then, all of your prayers suddenly kick in. Suddenly, the thorns begin to unravel. Suddenly, the thistles begin to be removed. With tears in their eyes, they repent of their sins and accept Christ. You are sitting in Heaven, and see this and you think, "Wow, I had such a lack of faith all my life. I didn't believe in my own prayers. I was just complaining all the time that my prayers were not working." You did not realize that your prayers were working. They were just in time, when the time came.

Thorns and thistles can be poverty. There are thorns and thistles in many countries due to the sin of governments. You see it in whole countries. In fact, sometimes you ask yourself the question, "How can I redeem the land if I am trying to redeem myself?" And then you rationalize, "I have a calling, but I have a problem. I have a calling, but this [situation] in my life probably disqualifies me." Can you relate to this? So can I. I am not superman in the spirit. I am not the super Christian. I too am fighting the enemy on a regular basis. So let me encourage you. Sometimes God allows certain things to happen in our lives to bring us to a place of humility, so that we can bear the image of the great intercessor, Jesus Christ.

Sometimes God allows circumstances, and you say, I prayed that this thorn would be removed. Paul prayed that way. "I prayed to God three times that He would remove this thorn." II Corinthians 12:7-9.

Can you imagine the Apostle Paul? He asked for the thorn and the thistle to be removed, yet God did not remove it. He asked for that thorn to be removed three times. God said this, "My grace is sufficient for you." God says the same things to us, "My grace is sufficient for you."

Why does God allow it? It is all part of intercession. **Sometimes God allows things to keep us on our knees.** Sometimes God allows things to always remind us that we are in the flesh and that we need His grace. Sometimes the grace you need to redeem the land you can only access through a certain level of humility. So, He has to keep you humble. My mentor once said to me, "God needs your imperfections as much as He needs your perfections." He began to show me this in the Bible. Every Bible hero had something. They had some crisis they went through. They had some time of crying out to God in desperation – the prophets, everybody! Sometimes when God wants to use you in intercession you find yourself in a garden sweating on a rock, and crying out to God. You find yourself saying, "If possible would you pass this cup of intercession to someone else? Can I avoid this cup?" Then, you say in your heart, not my will but Your will! (Luke 22:42).

Imagine Jesus, going to the cross, and He is beaten. He is mocked. He is whipped. Thorns and thistles are put on His head. He goes through all of this and yet He is righteous, He is perfect. He is more perfect than you and I and He is going through worse. They take Jesus, they hang Him on a cross. He is righteous and He takes on the image of your sin (1 John 3:5).

The whole Old Testament was speaking about the savior that will come. This savior is going to win the world. He is the conquering king. At the height of His victory, victory looked like a man hanging half naked, bloody and beaten, on a cross. It did not look glorious. He was not even up there alone, as a martyr. He was up there with two common thieves! The Bible says He was numbered with the transgressors (Luke 22:37). The height of victory for the Kingdom of God, looked like that!

The Bible says that when Jesus died He spent three days in the heart of the earth (Matthew 12:38-45). We believe He went down to Hell (Hades) because He had to pay the full price that you and I had to pay because of our sin. He goes into the heart of the earth. Hell receives Him gladly because He looks like sin. He snatches back the keys of authority and then He is raised from the dead. Now He has the keys of authority. The authority to redeem the man. The authority to redeem the woman. The authority to redeem the land. He then ascends and sits down at the right hand of the Father. The One who sits down at the right hand has the authority.

The Bible says you are seated with Him. You are with Him in Heavenly places, in authority (Ephesians 2:6). You are with Him with authority, with those keys to redeem men, redeem women, and redeem the land.

On what basis do we have this authority? It is because of Jesus – Jesus had the crown (Matthew 27: 29). He took the thorns and thistles, which represented the curses of the earth and they pressed them into His head. He wore them like a crown. All of hell laughed. The Roman soldiers laughed. He looked foolish wearing a crown of thorns. They did not understand. Jesus' crown of thorns declared uncontested, "I am King over your curses! I am King over the land! I am King over your poverty! I have authority over your poverty! I have authority over your sickness! I can relieve your sickness! I can redeem your situation! I am King over the curses!

They said, "He's a king; a king needs a scepter." (Matthew 27:29). The king needs a scepter, so they pulled a reed out of the ground. They took a reed from the land and placed it in His hands. "Look how funny He looks!" Imagine people passing by, "That man says He's a king? Look at how weak He is. Look at how funny He is." That man says he is a pastor? Look at his life. That person says they are called to redeem the land? Look at all they are going through. What kind of king is that? They did not realize that the reed in His hand was a prophetic picture of a scepter. A scepter in a king's hand is very important. It represents authority. **A scepter is also a tool that a king uses to commission people.** Jesus was saying, "I am a king. I have authority. I am gaining authority by the things of which I suffer. It doesn't look to the world that I am successful. It doesn't look to the world that I am qualified. I gained authority through the things which I suffered. I can commission now the body of Christ with My scepter."

I have seen this in the life of my mentor. The more he suffered, the more sons and daughters he raised up. Sometimes you see the results right away. Sometimes you are going to wait to see them from Heaven. You will be in the great cloud of witnesses and you will say, "Ah, that is why God let me go through that. That is why this happened to me." God will say, "You thought it was going to last forever." Jesus says to you, "That thing that you were praying for, it just happened! It just happened! You got the victory!" Paul will also say, "Those thorns in my side kept me as an intercessor, which gave me more authority."

Lastly, it was important that Jesus died on a cross. There was something very significant about the way He died. **Nothing God does is by chance.** When they lifted Him up on a cross, they planted that tree, that cross in the ground! It was almost like when you climb a mountain. You climb Mt. Everest and when you get to the top to declare victory to the world, you plant a flag in the ground. It is a flag representing your country. "We climbed Everest. We have the victory." You put that flag in the ground! The same way as Jesus hung on that cross. People would walk by and say, "Wow, Caesar has got Him! The execution has happened." Jesus, however, hung there like a flag for the Kingdom of God, declaring the redemption of man, and the redemption of the land!

It is amazing to me the people that God uses and the things that keep them humble. When Satan sends some things your way, you need to rebuke them. Do not just accept things from the devil. There are some things that for some reason God has not removed. You have done everything you know how to do. Even then you blame yourself. Yet God is doing something through you. I said to Him, "Thank God He could trust you with that crisis."

You really want to redeem the land? Can God trust you with problems? Can God trust you with thorns? He could trust Jesus with thorns.

Jesus went all the way. Are you willing to trust God with your own death and tribulations that you go through? Are you willing to trust that He will even raise you from the dead after the hard time is over? This is intercession that redeems the land!

Amazing! Can God trust you with the thorns and thistles in your life? Can you take it by faith today that the things God has not lifted off of you yet, can He trust you? Can you believe that your intercession is accomplishing something?

If you can begin to inject faith into that, if you can give your struggles and humility tests over to God, and if you can give your pain over to God, God can redeem much through that trouble.

Isaiah 43:1-4

But now, thus says the Lord, your Creator, O Jacob, And He who formed you, O Israel, "Do not fear, for I have redeemed you; I have called you by name; you are Mine! When you pass through the waters, I will be with you; And through the rivers, they will not overflow you. When you walk through the fire, you will not be scorched, Nor will the flame burn you. For I am the Lord your God, The Holy One of Israel, your Savior; I have given Egypt as your ransom, Cush and Seba in your place. Since you are precious in My sight, Since you are honored and I love you, I will give other men in your place and other peoples in exchange for your life."

No matter what you go through, you belong to Him. He can do what He wants to! Some people see the promise that He will be with you. Do you know what the currency is that God uses to reach people? He uses your life, surrendered to Him – willing to sacrifice for others. What this Scripture says is that your life has value. You are so valuable to God. Your life and your life alone is precious in God's eyes. In fact, it says, it is honored. Your life is of such high value to God, that whatever you suffer or sacrifice for the sake of reaching nations, God must compensate you for your suffering! God must compensate your suffering and sacrifice with something of equal value to your life or greater. If you have to endure pain, persecution, even seasons of prayer, seasons of fasting – God will reward you. What does He reward you with? Often we think that the compensation He gives us is material gain, like money, cars, etc. If God were to reward you with these things He would be devaluing you! God's compensation for your sacrifice must be something worthy of the value of your life – something of equal value to your life.

You see? God wants to reward you with nations! People groups! The very people for whom you are laying your life down in intercession or even tangible persecution – those souls become your reward! Cush and Seba are yours! This is a principle in the economy of God. Who you lay your life down for, God will reward you with. This is a principle of intercession and reaching nations. This is actually why God was able to say to His son Jesus, "Ask and I will give the nations as your inheritance" (Psalm 2:8). Your inheritance is always connected to souls!

When Jesus sat down, having paid such a high price. God said, "Okay Jesus, I trusted You with thorns. I trusted You with thistles. Now, ask Me and I will give You nations as Your inheritance."

You have not seen your future. Sometimes I see people living and behaving like they have no future. That is limiting God. Do you think this God that you serve is not going to compensate you? You do not even remember the land. You are so obsessed with complaining and selfishness, that you do not realize the complaining, the negative words, the selfishness, and all, work against your intercession. They work against what God is trying to do.

As surely as you have sown you will reap!

Deuteronomy 16:20

Justice, and only justice, you shall pursue, that you may live and possess the land which the Lord your God is giving you.

When we are ending injustice we are participating in a form of intercession. Our actions on behalf of justice make the world a better place. We are bringing the Gospel to a lost and dying world.

Activation Points:

1. Other than prayer, what else is necessary to redeem the land?

2. How do we know that we have been given authority to establish the Kingdom anywhere and everywhere?

3. Explain the Scripture found in Proverbs 13:23. What is this really saying?

4. Is it possible for the land to be cursed? Prove your answer by providing Scripture.

5. Explain the significance of Jesus' crown of thorns, the reed in His hand, and His cross in the ground, as it pertains to redeeming the land.

CHAPTER SIXTEEN:

INTERCESSION TO DELIVER CITIES AND NATIONS

True intercession is absolutely critical to changing even one heart, much less the world. Without intercessors, the earth might have succumbed to Satan's desires centuries ago. It is how we get a hold of God. It is how we get ourselves and our church lined up with His Word and His will. If there is no intercession, there is no revival. If there is no intercession the changes we are talking about, bringing the Kingdom of Heaven to earth is impossible.

Let's start by looking at Scripture.

Colossians 2:15

When He had disarmed the rulers and authorities, He made a public display of them, having triumphed over them through Him.

It is important to disarm a principality or power. You think when you go to war that you always have to use a certain amount of force. Sometimes to disarm something, you just need to cut one wire. Sometimes disarming is very meticulous, using just the right key. Can you believe the Bible talks this way? Jesus hung on the cross and disarmed rulers and authorities. He did not just do that, He put them to open shame. He humiliated them.

The humiliation was this, that they would not be able to have any effect. Do not think about destroying Satan. Instead, think about disarming him, so that no matter what he may try, he will have no effect.

Too often we want to win our battles in a hurry. This is understandable. Often though, this is not the way with spiritual warfare. Spiritual warfare is about much more than quick brute force. It is about obtaining the victory that Jesus won on the cross and bringing that moment in history into the situation you are fighting at any given moment. Jesus has won the victory. Our prayers are such that they bring that victory from the spiritual realm to the physical realm.

We are also guilty of looking at intercession and spiritual warfare as if it were some type of deep magic. Nothing could be further from the truth. As we have been studying, there are laws and principles in the natural world. There are laws such as gravity that cannot be defied. We are always subject to the law of gravity. Even our rockets that go into space are defined by the law of gravity. **We had to develop engines that had so much power that they could lift an object from the face of the earth, not by defying gravity, but rather by overcoming gravity with a stronger law of physics.**

In the same way, there are spiritual laws that are just as strong and controlling as gravity. They are not overcome with magic. They are overcome with a stronger law of the spiritual realm. That is what the work of Jesus on the cross is about.

Intercession opens up the spiritual world so that the higher laws of God can take place in the lives of men and women who have, until now, been bound by the laws of nature and nature's false god, Satan. Like Jesus on the cross, intercessors are stepping into eternity to bring eternity into time and space. They are stepping into eternity on behalf of communities and nations and people, changing the world by setting people free from the power of principalities and power.

What higher calling could there ever be for a Christian?

Luke 11:20

But if I cast out demons by the finger of God, then the kingdom of God has come upon you.

This reveals a very important principle. There is never the absence of kingdoms. If one kingdom is absent the other one is present. If the kingdom of darkness is present it means the Kingdom of Light is absent. When the Kingdom of Light is present, the kingdom of darkness is absent. This is very simple. Wherever you see the most human depravity and darkness, it means there is no presence of light. So, the work we have to do is to dispel darkness. We uproot a kingdom so that another kingdom can come in. This is your job – this is our job!

Remember, there is actually no such thing as darkness. Darkness is merely the absence of light. The way to defeat darkness in a room is to bring light into it. You do not have to labor to cast out the darkness when you bring the light. The harder part is bringing light. It is no work for light to dispel darkness. The work is getting the light to the darkness. Even a dim light will cast darkness from a room, even though it leaves shadows.

Our job as intercessors is to help bring the light. It is not to cast out darkness. You see, casting out darkness is the job of the light. Any time light is present darkness is gone. They cannot exist in the same room. There is no such thing as a room that is half-light and half-darkness. The room is either darkness or light. So, when you are interceding, intercede to bring the light. Bind the strongman, but bind him so that the light can come. Destroy the armor so that light can come.

Light in the physical world is love in the spiritual world. Perfect love casts out fear (1 John 4:18). Fear destroys man. Fear causes us to not reach our true potential. Fear causes us to turn back right before we achieve our goals. Fear causes us to settle for where we are. So, when you are praying for the light to cast out the darkness, you are really praying for the love of God to come to any situation. Love defeats all enemies. Love overcomes sin. Love overcomes anxiety. Love overcomes hate. Love is the victor in all things. The greatest of these is love.

For someone to identify properly their place of calling and step into intercession, an encounter with God is important. Carve out time for this and take a season of prayer.

This simply means, take more than just a morning or more than just a day in prayer. Be fervent in seeking God for an encounter and the revelation of your calling. Do not rush through this time with God, but be patient and willing to spend the time needed to have this encounter. Here is a Scriptural reference of this season to help you understand the process you are going to go through.

Ezekiel 1:28

As the appearance of the rainbow in the clouds on a rainy day, so was the appearance of the surrounding radiance. Such was the appearance of the likeness of the glory of the Lord. And when I saw it, I fell on my face and heard a voice speaking.

A true encounter with God should always reveal something to you, or you should HEAR something.

What He reveals will be somehow connected to His purpose for you. For example, the first thing God showed me as a pastor was the state of the church. He needed me to have a deep understanding of the church's condition in order for me to understand the apostolic calling of a planter on my life, so that I would step into my purpose – the reformation of the local church.

Ezekiel 2:1-3

Then He said to me, "Son of man, stand on your feet that I may speak with you!" As He spoke to me the Spirit entered me and set me on my feet; and I heard Him speaking to me. Then He said to me, "Son of man, I am sending you to the sons of Israel, to a rebellious people who have rebelled against Me; they and their fathers have transgressed against Me to this very day."

After every deep encounter with God some kind of commission or responsibility should come from it.

A commission is a CONTINUING word. In this verse, you can clearly see that Ezekiel was commissioned. He was given an assignment and sent. We clearly see that God tells Ezekiel who He is sending him to and the state of the people He is sending Ezekiel to reach. This is a very clear commission born of an encounter with God. **If you are desiring to fulfill your calling (or purpose), do not pray for God to do it for you, pray and ask God, "Who will You send me to and what is the state of the people?"**

Ezekiel 3:1-4

Then He said to me, "Son of man, eat what you find; eat this scroll, and go, speak to the house of Israel." So I opened my mouth, and He fed me this scroll. He said to me, "Son of man, feed your stomach and fill your body with this scroll which I am giving you." Then I ate it, and it was sweet as honey in my mouth. Then He said to me, "Son of man, go to the house of Israel and speak with My words to them."

Before God will entrust you with a ministry to others, you must eat the scroll and drink the cup of INTERCESSION.

This is a very important illustration. It is amazing that when we receive a Word from God (eat the scroll), it is truly sweet like honey to the taste. It always feels good and it is a sweet experience to hear from God. In fact, we will walk out of our prayer closets so excited that He has commissioned us.

What we often forget, however, is that once we have to do the intercession (drink the cup), that same commission becomes bitter in the stomach. This kind of prayer and intercession literally "fills your body with the scroll" that God gave you. Intense prayer and intercession is the price that few people are willing to pay to reach the people God has called them to reach. This kind of encounter with God is an important one. It is here that He not only reveals your purpose (your assignment) to you, but also fully equips and enables you to complete it. He provides you with His Word that will be your daily bread and sustenance, your reference and your rock, your sword, and your shield as you walk in your purpose.

You are now called and equipped for intercession. This is the place of battle and it is the place where the battle is won. Many make the mistake of entering into the natural-realm fight without having first battled in the Spirit-realm for the sure victory. My friend, welcome to the battlefield of spiritual warfare. It is okay, you need not be afraid. God's Word, the scroll you have already eaten, has been given to you. You have what you need to win.

Intercession is absolutely necessary so do not skim over the following verses but take the time to read them, meditate on them, understand them and become well versed in using them.

Joel 3:9

Proclaim this among the nations: Prepare a war; rouse the mighty men! Let all the soldiers draw near, let them come up! Beat your plowshares into swords and your pruning hooks into spears;
Let the weak say, "I am a mighty man."

Isaiah 43:3-4

"For I am the Lord your God, the Holy One of Israel, your Savior; I have given Egypt as your ransom, Cush and Seba in your place. Since you are precious in My sight, since you are honored and I love you, I will give other men in your place and other peoples in exchange for your life.

II Samuel 22:48

The God who executes vengeance for me, and brings down peoples under me,

Only when prayer and intercession have cost you the value of your life can God give you lives in exchange for your life. You become a deliverer.

Luke 11:20-22

"But if I cast out demons by the finger of God, then the kingdom of God has come upon you. When a strong man, fully armed, guards his own house, his possessions are undisturbed. But when someone stronger than he attacks him and overpowers him, he takes away from him all his armor on which he had relied and distributes his plunder."

Now what does binding the strongman have to do with fulfilling your purpose? We have to understand that in the earthly realm, every sphere of influence is being influenced by some kind of kingdom. It is either (a) the Kingdom of God and Light, or (b) the kingdom of Satan and darkness. Wherever one kingdom is absent, another one is sure to be present. In fact, this is why some areas of society, even some parts of your city or nation, are worse than others. This is not just a coincidence or natural phenomenon. This is due to the fact that we "wrestle not against flesh and blood." In Luke 11:20-22, Jesus gives a very powerful illustration that helps us to go beyond basic prayer into strategic prayer. I can remember a time in my ministry where I became frustrated, I wanted to see results beyond the four walls of the church, yet it seemed so difficult to get anything functioning in our community. We had no problem seeing God move in our church, but beyond our church, the ground seemed hard and the Heavens seemed brass. Out of pure desperation, I decided to make myself homeless in the street for three days. I would live there, sleep there, eat there, and pray for breakthrough in our community.

I can vividly remember the first day I began prayer walking downtown, and within about a half an hour, I had run out of things to pray about. I had done all the binding of the strongman

I could do, yet I was left with the question, "Is this really effective?" and even a sense of fear as to whether arousing this strongman would cause him to retaliate against me. I really had more questions than answers, and certainly did not feel that I had bound the strongman that was over our city. It was at this point, the first evening, that the Lord had mercy on me, and gave me a revelation from Luke 11:20-22.

As long as we bind a strongman who is fully armed, we really do not take much ground against him; we are certainly not able to plunder his goods, and if anything, he receives all our yelling and binding as worship and attention. Imagine your words being arrows that bounce off his armor and fall to the ground? This actually explains why many well-meaning believers and leaders who attempt to dethrone principalities end up being the loser in that battle. Some give up because of exhaustion, some give up not seeing the results they were hoping for, while others fall into strange sicknesses or even see their family obliterated; even though we read in the Bible that they have authority. This was the difficult road I was heading down when I began to pray for my city. But that first night I asked the Holy Spirit an important question: just what is the armour of the strongman and how can we remove it? It was then that Holy Spirit began to educate me in the strategy Jesus was alluding to. The armor that gives a strongman legal rights over a family, city, or even a nation, are the sins of that people group. Sin always gives the enemy legal access. The sins of a person or people group is the armor that holds the strongman in place; and unfortunately sin does not evaporate. Sin remains as do curses until the blood of Jesus washes it white as snow.

The problem is, for the blood of Jesus to be accessed to break curses, there must be repentance. What do you do if a person, people group, city, or nation will not repent? This is where

217

intercession is so crucial. This is where God looks for a man or He looks for a woman to "stand in the gap."

God looks for someone to repent on behalf of the sins of the people and bridge the gap between them and the God who blesses. Once I discovered this on that first night, prayer became endless. Immediately the Holy Spirit opened my eyes to see the sins of our city. I suddenly saw people doing things I never noticed them doing before. My eyes were opened to the alcoholism, drug addiction, prostitution, and corruption that was in our city. Not only did the Lord open my eyes to see these things, He actually gave me His heart concerning the people of this city. He turned my praying into weeping, and my weeping became a deep intercession, that led to great repentance for the sins of my city.

I began to repent on behalf of people of the community, our local churches, our city leaders, and anyone who the Holy Spirit brought to my mind. I walked to different parts of the city writing down in a journal the sin I was seeing. Not so that I could judge the people of our city or preach against them in some sermon on a Sunday morning, but so that I could accurately repent on behalf of the people who did not yet know God. What I discovered was, when you repent of sin, you remove the strongman's armor and legal access in a family, city, or nation. This is the principle of intercession, and we see it in the life of Moses, who prayed on behalf of Israel and then God had mercy on Israel. We also see this principle throughout the Bible, but ever more clearly through our Lord Jesus Christ – our Lord who hung on a cross and repented on our behalf as a people who did not know God.

Repentance strips the strongman's armor right off his body. Once you get a sense from the leadership of the Holy Spirit that your prayers have done significant work in this area, you can move on to binding and loosing. In this order, you are able to bind demonic powers because they no longer have "armor to rely on." That is when the full measure of a believer's power of authority can be seen. At this point in the game, when you bind and loose, it is as the Scriptures say, "Whatever you bind will have been bound in Heaven and whatever your loose on earth will have been loosed in Heaven."

Essentially this means you will be an accurate marksman with the prayers that you pray, and the enemy has no choice but to let go of that family, city, or nation. Period! Automatically then the kingdom of darkness is dethroned and another kingdom rushes in, the kingdom of our Lord Jesus Christ. Suddenly that people group that you have laid your life down for in prayer come under the blessing of King Jesus.

After those three days of prayer on the street, I began to see immediate change. We actually were able to start the very first Transformation Council. The different individuals on the council began extraordinary work, and had extraordinary grace and impact on our communities. Some were featured on TV for their social work, while others were promoted to prominent positions in the community. One thing was for sure, all of them were seeing the results of successful and effective ministries in which it seemed Satan could not stop or hinder them. Over the following year and beyond, things began to take place in the city that went beyond the council. Of course the stories are too numerous to share here, but let's just say we were able to see this principle work wonders in our sphere of influence and the world.

The Gospel has the power to change every person it truly comes in contact with. The Gospel is so real that it will transform a nation. As long as we keep the Gospel bound up in our churches, we are basically lighting a candle and hiding it under a bushel basket. We have to do more. If we continue to operate under the old model we have been using, we need to expect that revival, reformation will not come. We cannot continue to repeat the same activities and expect to have a different result. Einstein called that insanity.

The church needs to step back from insanity and step into the sanity of the Gospel, the active Gospel that feeds the hungry, heals the sick, heals the broken hearted, gives shelter to the homeless, builds businesses within the community to support the street level work of the Gospel, and thus changes a town, a city, a Province, and ultimately a nation!

I needed to get this burden first. Then, I realized something else. God does not just want your church to worship Him. He wants the whole city to worship Him. When I realized that God's dream was to reach everyone, I thought, *"Wow, we do not even have enough church buildings for all of them."* I began to see that the need was great. The Bible says that the god of this world has blinded their eyes, so that they will not see (2 Corinthians 4:4). You can be talking to someone about Jesus, but if a strongman is in place, they often cannot grasp it. They do not want it. When a strongman is removed, people easily choose Jesus and receive salvation.

The Holy Spirit is trying to reveal Jesus to everybody. So if there is an absence of the revelation of Jesus Christ, it means darkness is in place and the strongman has a hold.

If I cast out demons by the finger of God, then the Kingdom of God has come upon you.

The fact that you are reading this, studying this message, means that God has called you to do this. God is doing this through you. God is calling you! God is training you! He is bringing you out of ignorance and into a reality that many other Christians do not have. They are too proud to have it, or too full. God is giving it to you!

There will be many lonely days and lonely nights if you are going to be an intercessor. There will be times when everyone is out doing something you would like to do, but you sense God telling you, "Now is the time to bind the strongman, tonight is the night of the breakthrough." So you stay behind, giving up the fun of this generation to change the course of the history of this generation. That is what intercession is about. It is "calling those things that are not, as though they were." It is binding what is bound in Heaven. It is loosing what is loosed in Heaven. It is about bringing God's Kingdom to earth, as it is in Heaven.

Activation Points:

1. Name seven positive attributes of your sphere of influence.

2. Explain how "eating the scroll" and "drinking the cup" relate to intercession.

3. Name seven sins that your sphere of influence needs to repent from. For example, if you are called to the area of arts and entertainment one of those sins might be taking the Lord's name in vain. Another sin might be belittling the name of Jesus through weak depictions of those of the Christian faith.

4. Set aside time to pray a prayer of repentance related to each of these sins listed above.

CHAPTER SEVENTEEN:

ORGANIZED THOUGHT – THE HIGHEST LEVEL OF POWER

When we think in terms of what an organized thought might be, we often end up confused. Maybe we would define it as thinking in an organized way. We might define it as strategic thinking. Organized thinking does encompass those things, but there is actually a more definitive answer for what organized thought is. There is a reason why it is actually so powerful and effective.

In fact, the very few who govern spheres of influence in society, those who are leaders, rulers, the ruling elite, they understand the power of organized thinking. The difference between someone building a large organization or company, a fortune 500 Company, and someone building a smaller company is the difference between having a dream or a vision and having an organized thought. We must develop the ability to think in an organized way. Any large company that you see succeeding and having influence, is because somebody in that company has learned to think in an organized way.

It is not just the great ideas that rise to the top of the business world. It can be the lesser idea that comes from a company that is incredibly organized and has a leadership team capable of organized thinking at a higher level It is not always the most talented who rise to the top. Often it is people of lesser talent who work in a more organized way, thinking creatively, building systems to further their cause.

Here is a definition of what an organized thought actually is: **A mental image within which you can see from beginning to end and the steps in between all at the same time.** It is the ability to see not just letter A and letter Z, but all of the other letters in between. **Organized thinking is the ability to see how to start something, how it should finish, and what steps you need to take to reach your end goals.**

As surprising as it is, few people ever approach their dreams with organized thought. They think that the dream drives everything. They think that as long as they push hard enough after the dream it will come to pass. After all, it is a dream that was likely given to them by God. Is it not true that God will work on our behalf to cause the dreams He has put in our heart to come to pass? This leaves them believing that the work is in God's hand, they merely have to dream the dream. Nothing could be further from the truth. There is a great amount of work that must go into any dream becoming reality.

If you are called to government service as an elected official, it is critical that you not just think that God will win the election for you. You must learn how to campaign. You must formulate policy positions on every area that the position you are seeking has influence over. You must go to meetings and speak about your plans, your ideas. You must develop a team of people around you who can support you in every area. You have to have someone to arrange your schedule. You have to have someone who travels with you to meetings and watches your back. You must have someone who can organize community outreaches for your cause. You have to have someone making sure you have written materials and signs for yards, bumper stickers for cars.

You have to have someone who understands marketing and how to get your message out in the most effective manner. And this is not the complete list!

So, in this one area you can see that while God is sovereign, it takes a lot of work on your part to actually achieve your dream. It is not enough for God to give you the dream. He expects you to do your part. That is where organized thought comes into play.

A man or nation, without an organized system of thought will always be at the mercy of the man or nation that has one.

Jim Collins book, "*From Good to Great,*" is a very thorough analysis of the key factors in companies and leaders who excelled. Excelled even in a time of economic drought. **First, they had disciplined people. Next, they had disciplined thinking. Finally, they had disciplined action.** You cannot have disciplined action unless you have disciplined thought. You cannot have disciplined thought without having disciplined people. These were some of the main ingredients that caused these companies to thrive.

It takes all three working in coordination for a company or a ministry to have success. One without the other two, or two without the final one, will never lead to greatness. It might lead you to a successful company or ministry, but we are talking about opportunities that change the world. We are not talking about settling for the world's view of success. Rather, we are talking about settling for God's view of success.

When it comes to dealing with nations, this is even more critical. We think we understand what it takes to lead a nation to greatness. We think it takes turning the nation to God through revival. It takes much more than great services or even prayer. Now, I am not downplaying the value of Christian gatherings or prayer here. What I am talking about is going beyond prayer into organized thinking. Organized thinking is required to lead a nation to greatness. It is required to set up systems that feed, clothe, provide water, and then develop the infrastructure necessary for smoothly operating on a daily basis.

Righteousness within a nation must be organized if it is to be enforced. You cannot just pray for a country to have righteousness. You have to organize systems that enforce righteousness to establish a system within a country, or even a company, that creates culture, you have to be organized in your establishment of that system. You cannot just have a good idea, share your idea, and hope it happens. You cannot share your vision and hope God comes down and does it. If you want to establish vision in a company and create culture anywhere you have to have a systematic way to do that and utilize systems to do that. You have to be organized first in your mind. You have to see beginning to end of how that system works, as well as the steps to get from the beginning to the end.

Power is not always where we think it is. Sometimes we think that power to accomplish something is just found in prayer, or just found in masses of people, but in actuality power is found in our ability to build systems. The power in a company is found in its ability to systematize itself. The power, even within a church, should be, not just Holy Ghost power, but it should be the ability to establish a system that enforces values that create culture. If you have values and principles that you want to establish in a city, or even in your home, it is important to set up routines and systems that make sure the principles and values are being adhered to. What creates culture are those things which allow us to be fruitful, multiply, fill the earth, and subdue it with the culture of Heaven.

Henry Ford is a great example of this. He did not invent the car. He merely developed a system for manufacturing cars that revolutionized the world at that time, and continues to revolutionize the world today. He developed the assembly line. This is a process where instead of one person building a car in a stationary position, the car moves down a line and different people have different jobs to build the car. So the chassis starts down the line. Someone puts in the seats. Someone puts in the steering wheel. Someone puts the dash assembly in. A different person or group of persons do different jobs along the way until at the end of the process there is a completed car. This took building a car from a long process for each car to hundreds and ultimately thousands of cars being built in the course of a day!

This is revolutionary organized thinking that is capable of changing the world!

On the other end of the scale there are companies, ministries, even nations and continents that are so disorganized that they never come close to reaching their potential. They never achieve the calling of God in their life.

Africa is a continent of many countries that is hugely rich in raw materials and resources. Yet, they are not able to utilize these resources because of their lack of systems and honor of Biblical values. Proper systems in place and organized thinking would make a huge difference in Africa. Plus, organized crime and corruption actually hinders Africa, as a whole, becoming what it could be – truly rich and great! I would go as far as saying that some first world countries are actually afraid of Africa becoming organized. They are afraid that if Africa rises they will lose their place as a leading nation.

As a result, Africa does not have clean running water or electricity in many places. They do not have good transportation systems. They have economies that do not provide for the people. All of this is because of poor systems. They have the richest continent in the world in terms of natural resources. **It is not enough to have riches; you must have systems to distribute those riches in a way that causes the country to prosper.**

This is why there is fear of nations like China and Japan. Because of their ability to build systems. That is one of the reasons that Japan's economy is doing so well. It is because of the systems that enforce their values and culture. This is to say that the world does not belong to the most spiritual. It belongs to the most organized. The race is not won by the swift (Ecclesiastes 9:11). The contest is not won by the most talented. It is won by the most organized.

This teaching does not compute in the mind that was raised in a western Sunday School. We were raised in the church in a culture that was at the height of its success. There were assumptions made that led us to where we are. Prior organized thinking has made us great. Over the past few decades, we have deteriorated to the point of being a country run by regulations instead of organized thinking. This is one of the problems with building systems. When the original thinkers are gone, they are often replaced with bureaucrats who think the system is a naturally occurring thing. They believe that they have to keep the system going no matter what. Even when the system becomes outdated because of changing circumstances, they keep it going.

We have to relearn how to build churches that change the world. We have to relearn how to build ministries and outreaches that change the world. We have to relearn how to engage the culture in ways that will make a difference in the lives of the people.

Even the church, though it is the epicenter of the Kingdom of God on earth; even the church, though it is called the wisdom of God to all principalities of darkness and evil; even the church which is an example to nations... – even the church, rises on its ability to be organized, or falls because of its disorganization. That is why you can meet many spiritual people who are not having success, because they are not organized. On a Sunday morning you can walk into spiritual churches that are not discipling nations or impacting their communities because of their lack of organization.

Proverbs 13:23

Abundant food is in the fallow ground of the poor, But it is swept away by injustice.

This means that anyone, anywhere, even the poor could prosper. Even the fallow ground of the poor could produce much fruit but it is swept away by injustice. Replace the word injustice with the word disorganization. God sees disorganization and injustice as one in the same. If there is injustice on the planet earth there is also poverty and corruption, He sees it as the earth being disorganized. So they are one and the same. If you are telling your child to go clean up his room you could say, "Go bring justice to your room." So, disorganization is essentially an injustice in God's eyes, and it needs to be an injustice in our eyes.

Even the poor could prosper, but their potential is swept away by disorganization. This means that anyone, anywhere can have success. Anyone, anywhere can prosper. Everyone has an equal opportunity to do well in their sphere and according to their standards. If they are disorganized they will lose their opportunity, or it will never reach its full potential. It is not a lack of God, it is not a lack of gift mix, most of us came into this world with two arms, two eyes, two ears. We all have opportunity, but what studies show is that prosperity is not based on what you have or do not have. **Prosperity is based on how you think.** If you are an organized thinker and you think in terms of organization and are disciplined enough to enact it from point A to Z, you can prosper. Even if you are poor, you can prosper. However, the opportunities are swept away by injustice in the form of disorganization.

The power to prosper in any field of life begins with your ability to think in an organized way. The principle is this: **the man who has learned to manage himself and be organized is qualified to manage something else.** All of this begins with organized thinking.

One of the problems with disorganized thinking is that it leads to chaos. Without organized thinking, we are limited in how big or how powerful something can become. Disorganized thinking might work in a "mom and pop shop," and there is nothing wrong if your vision is to own a family run restaurant or store, but it will not allow that same "mom and pop shop" operation to become a chain store or a franchise.

Chaos is found in the absence of good leadership. Disorganized thinkers are not always good leaders. They may have great ideas. They may have big plans. They may be the most inspirational person you have ever met. At the end of the day, however, they are not capable of inspiring for long periods of time because their plans never seem to come to pass.

The best example of organized thinking is God. I know this seems obvious, but let's look at the creation of the world. God called forth the earth, and everything that is in it, from chaos. Genesis says the earth was formless and void (Genesis 1:2). Out of the chaos of formlessness and void, God created everything. He also created it in such a way that the whole of the Universe operates as a system that supports itself. He created it according to scientific principles that have governed since the beginning of time until now. He had a plan. He had a good idea. He went about developing it according to a system that was sustainable. What better example could we hope for, than following the path of the God of the Universe!

The next principle is: **when better people refuse to be organized the worst people of society will rule.** That is to say, when righteous people refused to be organized, using self-management and systems, the worst of people, who are better organized, will rule. This is why the church has been so ineffective for so long. We are very spiritual people, but often we are very disorganized people. We will excuse our disorganization in the name of spirituality.

We even have a saying for this. "He is so Heavenly minded that he is no earthly good." That is what we are talking about here. We are talking about being both Heavenly minded and earthly good. The dreams and the visions come from Heaven. **The great ideas come from Heaven.** Every positive human achievement that has advanced and improved the lives of humans has come from the realm of Heaven. They have come from people, some of whom did not know God personally, who were able to reach into the invisible realm and make something, that was only a thought, became a reality. This is not easy because it takes organized thinking at a level we seldom see.

Christians should be the most organized thinkers in the world. After all, we are sons and daughters of the Most High God. We are brothers and sisters of Jesus. How is it then that we do not excel in the area of organized thinking? I believe a lot of the problem comes because we think that every solution to every problem is only spiritual. This is to fail to understand the nature of the Universe. While every solution begins in the spiritual realm, it is our job to bring the spiritual realm into the natural realm.

This is the lesson of Jesus. Jesus always existed. He was with the Father in the beginning. Through Him the world was created. He could have remained in Heaven and been just as real as He is today. He had to come to earth, however, for us to be redeemed. It took Jesus, the spiritual being, becoming Jesus the natural person on the earth for us to know salvation. It is the same with any idea or plan. Our job is to take these ideas and plans from the spiritual realm where they are conceived into the natural world through a process much like childbirth.

There is a conception. There is an incubation period where the idea or plan develops. There is the painful process of birthing the plan or the idea. Then you have to raise the plan or idea like a child until it is mature. All of this process requires organized thinking if you are going to grow the plan or idea into a mature organization that is capable of sustaining itself.

This quote shows exactly what we are talking about, **"When men with moral values refuse to come together and be organized, they will pay the price for it by enduring the rule of the worst of men."**

This is one of the problems we have in government and politics today. The system is so corrupt that good people are not willing to participate in it. They avoid stepping into politics. They avoid running for office. As a result, we end up with people of lesser moral principle stepping up and running for office. Then we complain that there are no good politicians any more. We are suffering, not from a lack of good politicians, but from a lack of statesmen. We are suffering from a lack of statesman, because there are no people stepping up because they are afraid of the system.

Here is another quote: **"When men of ability, quality, and character refuse to seek leadership positions or political influence, others who are worse than them make rules over them."** One of the reasons we as believers do not often seek leadership positions is that we are afraid of the discipline it requires to be a leader. We are even afraid of the need to be organized to be a leader.

A leader must be more than a spiritual person; they must also be a disciplined person. Most of your spirituality will not create character within you. Discipline will create character within you. Character is needed to be an effective leader.

This is where Christians often fail when they do step up and run for public office. They have the spiritual qualities but they do not have the character. They find themselves in situations where they are forced to make impossible choices. Their lack of character means they choose the lesser of two evils, instead of refusing to play the game and finding a way to change the rules. The pressure of the position gets to them. They start to believe their own press. They find themselves in financial need. An opportunity presents itself to them that seems to resolve their problem(s). It is not really wrong, but neither is it altogether right. They forget the old saying that says, "Anything that is not quite right, is wrong!"

Another shortcoming is that power is an aphrodisiac. Many people in power find themselves being seduced by their followers. I have seen this even with great pastors. If they do not have strong character, they will find themselves justifying having an affair with a young woman who is also a Christian and drawn to their power. The opportunity presents itself. There are a million reasons why it is a good thing. There is only one reason why it is a bad thing and that reason is spiritual rather than natural. Nature wins. Then, we witness the destruction of a family and a career, if not worse.

An organized lifestyle is necessary to be an effective leader. Why does God allow life to work like this? It seems like an injustice that organized heathens seem to be able to prosper more than spiritual believers. Why is this? The Bible says the earth has been given to the sons of men, according to Psalm 115:16. For God to truly love people He cannot be a dictator. God's greatest expression of love is seen in His ability to give us free will.

Since we have free will, we can choose to live and adhere to the laws and principles of life. Or we can neglect them. That is to say that there are laws and principles that govern spirituality and they allow mankind to be spiritual and even get to Heaven if they want to. Then, there are laws and principles that govern the earth realm, that allow unspiritual people to prosper and be successful on earth if they want to. Wouldn't it be great if those who are spiritual and on their way to Heaven could also abide by the laws and principles that allow them to succeed on earth?

That is how you bring the Kingdom of God effectively to earth. Jesus did not say, "I pray that everyone goes to Heaven." He did not pray that everyone will get the Kingdom after they die and go to Heaven. No, He said, "I pray Your Kingdom come on earth, Your will be done on earth, as it is in Heaven." (Mathew 6:10). Essentially, we are ambassadors and conduits for bringing Heaven to earth. We have gotten pretty good at bringing Heaven to our church buildings once a week. It is time, however, to establish Heaven in the business sector, to establish Heaven in the educational sector, to establish Heaven in our families, Heaven in arts and entertainment, Heaven in media, Heaven in every sphere of society. You have got to uphold the principles of the Kingdom. The only way you are going to be able to do that is through organized thinking and the establishment of systems that infuse the culture of Heaven into darkened culture here on earth, in every one of those mountains.

The idea is that it is time that the church, we Christians, stood up and began to have influence in every portion of society. It is time for us to get our hands dirty in politics, the media, the business world, education, arts and entertainment, literally every sphere, and bring the Kingdom of Heaven to earth. This has been God's plan from the beginning. We have spiritualized it to the place where we think that God's commandment to Adam and Eve to subdue the earth was about nothing more than the actual Garden of Eden. Or we believe that the commandment is not meant for us. Nothing could be further from the truth.

God has called us to make a difference. He has called us to use our calling and our gifts to change the portion of the world where we have influence. It is not easy because God has gifted us. In fact, in many ways it is harder because God demands so much of us when we step out into public life. Nonetheless, we are called and we must answer the call or fail God at a time when we are needed like never before.

This is essentially why it is not large megachurches that transform nations. It is small groups of people that actually influence the direction of nations. We have seen this in our own country with the underground, very covert operating, homosexual agenda. Homosexuals who were not wanting anything to do with Christianity, who had an agenda to change the laws of the land, have been working at it for years. They have worked in a very organized way. Part of their agenda was to make you believe that there were more homosexuals in our country than there actually were. They did not pray this into being. They started putting homosexual characters into key roles in television programs and movies. So, slowly, over time, we bought into the lie that homosexuality was everywhere. Not only everywhere, but that it was normal. Once you see something and hear a lie long enough you actually begin to believe it as the truth.

One thing we know as Christians is that truth is not relative. **What is true in this generation must have been true in every generation.** Man does not get to determine what is true and what is not true. Just like we can believe that gravity does not matter. That does not change the fact that if we step off the top of a ten story building, we are going to fall to the ground, hard. The truth of gravity is not dependent on our believing in the truth. It merely is. The same is true of spiritual truths. Morals do not change from one generation to the next. God has always had a code for man to live by. The fact that we do not believe in the code does not make the code any less real or true.

The change in the morality of homosexuality took place in a very organized way. Amazingly, a small percentage in America changed how the whole country feels about homosexuality. This happened while the vast majority, 70% of Americans, are professing Christians.

The balance of the direction of nations gets tipped based upon the ability of a small group of people to become an organized critical mass. Margaret Mead understood this. She is an American anthropologist who was responsible for the sexual revolution. She had a great understanding of sociology though she was not saved. She said, "Never doubt that a small group of thoughtful, committed citizens can change the world. Indeed, it is the only thing that ever has."

Essentially you could say, "Do not doubt that a small group of believers who are organized and have an organized system of thinking can change the world." These are the only kinds of people who ever do change the world.

This is why believers can be on their way to Heaven, but be absolutely incompetent when it comes to establishing the Kingdom of God in different spheres of influence.

Ecclesiastes 10:5-7

There is an evil I have seen under the sun, like an error which goes forth from the ruler, folly is set in many exalted places while rich men sit in humble places. I have seen slaves riding on horses and princes walking like slaves on the land.

This is the key to understanding when an author or a king says that "there is an evil I have seen under the sun," he is separating two dimensions. One is the dimension above the sun which is the spirit realm. The other is the dimension beneath the sun which is the earth realm. This king is saying that he has seen a law of life under the sun. He has seen a generality and a consistency of something, a law and principle under the sun, as if it were an error proceeding from a ruler. It is as if God had made a mistake – as if the creator of that dimension had made a mistake. It appears to be an injustice. It says, "Folly is set in many high places and the rich sit in low places."

I want us to focus on verse seven where he sees slaves on horses and princes walking on the ground like slaves. He means that he has seen the unrighteous riding on horseback like pompous princes just riding by, while he is seeing actual princes having to walk on the ground like slaves. What this means is that he has seen the unrighteous riding horses and succeeding, while the righteous are walking on the ground like slaves, barefoot. This is to say that the one who found a horse and knows how to use a horse is better off than the one who did not, regardless of their spirituality or righteousness.

Here we see the unrighteous is riding horseback and enjoying a smoother ride while the righteous person has to walk barefoot because of his lack of organization.

Would it not be amazing to see the Daniels rise up, the Josephs of our generation rise up? I doubt Joseph became Prime Minister because of his prayer life or even his righteousness. He must have known a few things. He must have known how to run the budget of a nation. He must have had wisdom. He must have understood organized thinking to prepare for famine, and how to exist in famine and be able to give to other nations.

Would it not be amazing to combine righteousness with organization? Would it not be amazing to have organized righteousness, instead of organized crime? This all begins with organized thinking. If we the righteous, we the spiritual, can combine God's level of organization, we will be able to be the head and not the tail. We will be able to disciple nations. We will be able to turn nations upside down for Jesus. We will be able to be the kings and judges of the earth, establishing righteousness to the degree that whole nations begin to identify themselves with King Jesus – then the Kingdom can come, and then ultimately Jesus can come.

This is the power of organized thinking. It can change nations! It can change continents! It requires discipline and character. It is harder than merely going along to get along. It is a place that requires diligence and study. Nonetheless, it is the place of our calling. If we want to be, who God has called us to be, then we have no choice but to learn how to think in an organized manner.

Activation Points:

1. What is the danger for the man/nation, who does not have his own organized system?

2. Why, according to Ecclesiastes 10:5-7 do princes walk while servants ride horses?

3. Why, according to Proverbs 13:23 do resources, riches, and blessings perish?

4. What do righteous people need to not do, to avoid becoming a victim in society?

5. Genesis 11:6-9 describes what power is concealed in the unity of righteous people?

Bibliography

Holy Bible: NASB. (1995). *New American Standard Bible (1995 Update)*. LaHabra, CA: The Lockman Foundation. As found in the Logos Bible study software program: https://www.logos.com.

For more information on becoming a part of The History Makers Academy, History Makers Society, or to schedule Pastor Derek Schneider, please visit: www.HistoryMakersAcademy.com

Resources by Derek Schneider

Available at:
www.Kingdom.com/HistoryMakersAcademy
www.HistoryMakersAcademy.AllChristian.net

Workshop Seminars:
History Makers Training DVDs complete with a Presenter at your church.

Disc 1 of 10: Session One – Part One
1. Introduction – Sowing the Seeds of Sons – PART ONE
2. Revival and the Harvest
3. Ekballo Experiences
4. How is This Affecting You?

Disc 2 of 10: Session One – Part Two and Session Two
1. Session One – Sowing the Seeds of Sons – PART TWO
2. Session Two – Self Enhancement Through Self Evaluation

Disc 3 of 10: Session Three
1. Session Three – Moral Maturity

Disc 4 of 10: Session Four
1. Session Four – Simulating Points of Pressure for High Performance Christianity

Disc 5 of 10: Session Five
1. Session Five – Life is Predictable

Disc 6 of 10: Sessions Six and Seven
1. Session Six – The Key to Resolving Every Problem and Achieving Every Goal
2. Session Seven – System Building to Guarantee Success

Disc 7 of 10: Session Eight
1. Session Eight – How to Create a Life Plan

Disc 8 of 10: Sessions Nine and Ten
1. Session Nine – Fighting Indiscipline

2. Session Ten – Meeting With Jesus
Disc 9 of 10: Session Eleven
    1. Session Eleven – Transformation of Culture: The Church's Ultimate Assignment
Disc 10 of 10: Session Twelve
    1. Session Twelve – The Undiscovered Power of Conversion – PART ONE
    2. Session Twelve – The Undiscovered Power of Conversion – PART TWO

Books:
Beyond The Four Walls
His Kingdom Your Purpose

Videos:
DVDs on the Kingdom by Derek Schneider
1. The Peculiarity of the Kingdom
2. The Church – The Platform for the Kingdom
3. What Gospel Are We Preaching?
4. Repentance – The Key to the Kingdom
5. Jesus: The Kingdom of God in Flesh
6. The Laws of the Kingdom – Part One
7. The Laws of the Kingdom – Part Two
8. A Kingdom Church
9. The Purpose of the Local Church
10. Bringing Forth the Fruit of the Kingdom
11. Redeeming the Land
12. The Absolutism of the Kingdom of God: The Revelation of the Church – Part One
13. The Absolutism of the Kingdom of God: The Revelation of the Church – Part Two
14. A Kingdom of Sons – Not a Kingdom of Slaves
15. The Seed of Significance in You
16. The Power of One
17. How to Get Results in the Kingdom